GREAT CANADIAN SPORTS STORIES

Trent Frayne & Peter Gzowski

GREAT
CANADIAN
SPORTS
STORIES

A
Century
of
Competition

The Canadian Centennial Library

Seven-man-a-side hockey at Victoria Rink, Montreal, in 1893. Photo was faked.

This volume designed by John Richmond

©

COPYRIGHT 1965

The Canadian Centennial Publishing Company Limited

ALL RIGHTS RESERVED

THE CANADIAN CENTENNIAL LIBRARY

WEEKEND MAGAZINE/McCLELLAND AND STEWART LIMITED

Pierre Berton, *Editor-in-Chief;* Frank Newfeld, *Art Director;* Ken Lefolii, *Managing Editor*

THE CANADIAN CENTENNIAL PUBLISHING COMPANY LIMITED

150 SIMCOE STREET, TORONTO, CANADA

Contents

SPORTS touch almost everyone, Queens and commoners alike.

It was Elizabeth II who insisted upon quitting the royal box at Toronto's Woodbine racetrack in the moments before the hundredth running of the Queen's Plate for a closer look at the thoroughbreds in the paddock. And when Lester B. Pearson, prime minister of Canada, turned up on the front pages of newspapers across the country just as his Liberal government was bringing down its third budget in the spring of 1965, it was not taxes that took him there; he was in a steamy dressing room wringing the perspiring paw of Charlie Hodge, a goalkeeper who had scored a Stanley Cup shutout. No other kind of television programme attracts the audience of the Saturday-night hockey game or the playoff football game. Even the sheltered physicist, baffled by the frenzy that attends the Grey Cup game, is apt to discover that his son knows the names and numbers of all the players.

Although sports touch almost everyone, not everyone wants to touch sports. A while back, a sportswriter friend of mine weighed an offer from another paper, and rejected it when his own publisher made a counter-proposal.

"We'll give you seventeen-five if you stay," the publisher said, "but we're not going to waste that kind of money on sports. From now on, you'll write for the editorial page."

All kinds of people take a patronizing view of sports, but it is fair to argue that they are either unrealistic – or the sort who hold an inflated notion of the importance of their own pursuits. It bears only passing mention, of course, that a lot of people *in* sports place an inflated value on their importance, too, but this can never be said of the ingredients that go into the making of a great athlete or a great team, which are as fundamental as life itself: courage, strength, a flair for competition, speed, teamwork, determination. Sports, as Herbert Warren Wind has written, can stir the complete man as can few other phases of life. When something is right in sports, few things are as beautifully right – Rocket Richard in full flight, the perfectly co-ordinated Stan Leonard hitting a golf ball, Bobby Hull swooping to his left, his right leg crossing high, or Marilyn Bell simply refusing to quit.

These are classic qualities and actions. William Hazlitt's eulogy of John Cavanagh, an early nineteenth-century master of a forerunner of handball called hand-fives, illuminated them more than a century ago. "When a person dies who does any one thing better than anyone else in the world, which so many others are trying to do well, it leaves a gap in society. It may be said that there are things of more importance than striking a ball against a wall – there are things, indeed, that make more noise and do as little good, such as making war and peace, making speeches and answering them, making verses and blotting them, making money and throwing it away. But the game of fives is what no one despises who has ever played at it . . . He who takes to playing at fives is twice young. He feels neither the past nor future in the instant. Debts, taxes, domestic treason, foreign levy, nothing can touch him further. He has no other wish, no other thought, from the moment the game begins, but that of striking the ball, of placing it, of *making* it!"

The thing about an athlete, any athlete, is his complete aloneness in being required to bring off his stuff in full view. If he is humiliated, his humiliation is total; he is derided not only by his enemies and his neighbours but – more and more in these days of television – by unseen millions. He never escapes this fishbowl as long as he plays his game, for, like the actor, he must climb into the white heat of the spotlight each time he picks up the tools of his trade and goes to

At his peak, Gordon Howe was the complete athlete. "All he had was – everything."

The game was born before the country was. On July 1, 1867, the Six Nations all-stars came to Toronto to see how well the local worthies could play lacrosse. The Indians won.

work. In competitive sports, as in few other places, there is no nepotic influence to permit the performer to learn the business, in the standard phrase, from the top down. And as he passes his prime there is no way for him to be booted safely upstairs to the sanctity of some high-sounding title. This may come later, if somebody upstairs likes him, but it happens only when the business side of sports takes over from the performing of them. This book is not concerned with the big-business aspect but with the people and the teams that performed during Canada's first hundred years, and with what made them perform the way they did.

It would be brazenly chauvinistic if a book dedicated to a century of sport in this country were to dwell entirely on the characteristics of great players and teams that are indigenous only to Canada. It would make for a very short book, too, because the elements that make for greatness are no more Canadian than they are American or Chinese or African – and no less so, either. The elements that produce the complete athlete are universal and, as we shall see, Canada has had her fair share of them in a hundred years of sport.

Still, there are certain aspects of our terrain and our climate and our history that have brought certain of our athletes to the international forefront, and these are the things that are *Canadian* about Canadian sports. Just as the all-year temperance of the east coast of Australia has produced, or at least influenced the development of, great swimmers and tennis players, and the dominating mountains of Austria have given that little country some of the world's most accomplished skiers, the cold demands of Canadian winters have bred all of the world's finest hockey players.

Hockey and curling are the only games in which great numbers of Canadians seriously compete, which is why, considered along with our climate, we are unequalled in hockey – and, of course, is why our only challenger in that game in the distant future may be Russia. I am speaking here, obviously, of our players in the National Hockey League, not of those who represent us, however bravely and even with a sort of gallant desperation, in the European tournaments and the Olympic Games, so unskilled and undernourished. Our great curlers – the Richardsons, Matt Baldwin, Hec Gervais and a legion of Manitobans before them – might as well have invented the game, so completely have they smothered all opposition for decades. In quite recent years, large numbers of Americans in the northern states have become addicted to this fast-growing game and in 1965, surprisingly, the U.S. won the world championship in Scotland for the first time – the first time, in fact, any country other than Canada has ever won it. But it would be folly to suggest that there are not more great curlers in our country than anywhere else in the world.

And we have been sufficiently endowed with the universal elements, as the ensuing chapters illustrate, that even in some of the sports where we have no right to expect international equality we have emerged from time to time as the best in the world – golf, swimming, rowing, boxing, basketball and, through the utterly unexpected recent development of a colt of the quality of Northern Dancer, thoroughbred racing. No one had more cool nerve than the speedboat driver Bob Hayward, no one was a greater strategist than Ned Hanlan. No one ever matched the bizarre feats of strength of Louis Cyr, few had the competitive flair of King Clancy or the capacity to endure of Marilyn Bell, and certainly no team ever dominated its game anywhere in the world with the precision and authority of the Edmonton Grads. Who ever rode a bike better than Torchy Peden or flicked a forehand faster than Jack Purcell when he was the world's greatest badminton player?

In the early years of the century, Canadians were restricted in their sports activities by their social, religious and economic status. Cricket and yachting flourished, straight from the British Isles and engaged in by most young gentlemen of means. D. M. Fisher noted in the *Canadian Forum* that almost all sports in Canada in the 1870s were organized by men from the military and business worlds and from the universities. Hockey and rugger were played in the universities, and the garrison towns – principally Montreal, Toronto and Halifax – organized lacrosse teams to play against Indian athletes. Hockey probably started in Kingston around 1855 when soldiers in the Royal Canadian Rifles tied skates to their boots, borrowed field-hockey sticks and began crashing into one another. When forwards lifted the puck instead of skimming it along the ice in shooting it, the men in goal borrowed wicket-keepers' leg guards from cricket to protect their assaulted shins.

These were the years for playing sports, rather than for watching them, and the terrain and the distance between communities and the climate shaped the nature of the games. Bicycle clubs featured intertown races along the dusty dirt roads on models whose front wheels were as high as a man's chest and back wheels scarcely as tall as his button-up boots. People were curling and speed-skating in competition on frozen Toronto Bay a full eight years before Confederation – one bonspiel there drew forty rinks in 1859. More than half a century earlier, in 1807, the first curling club in North America was organized by Scottish immigrants on the St. Lawrence River near Montreal. Snowshoeing was a major sport. In 1867 the Montreal Snow Shoe Club had a hundred and twenty-three members who staged overnight "tramps" during weekends and held regular race meetings that included obstacle jumps. Edwin C. Guillet, in *Early Life in Upper Canada*, writes that in winter months horse-racing on the frozen rivers and lakes was "a joy for everyone," excluding, presumably, the horses.

Spectator sports were by no means unknown, however. Lacrosse was so popular in the year of Canada's birth that it was made our national game by act of parliament. At that time, Indians played lacrosse summer and winter. In 1874 attempts were made by two white teams to play indoors on ice. (There had already been several such games outdoors.) The Crescents and the Victorias met in a Montreal rink, with players wearing skates. They used lacrosse sticks, and the hard rubber ball bounced and skidded so intemperately as to break three hundred dollars' worth of window panes.

Lacrosse had a role in fathering hockey. Late in 1870, the new game's rulemakers borrowed the goalposts of lacrosse as well as the idea of faceoffs and terms like referee and goal. (Lacrosse had been named by French settlers, who likened the cured webbed stick used by the Indians to a bishop's crozier.) William K. McNaught, president of the National Lacrosse Association in the middle 1870s, wrote of the dress of the players: "It has always been the fashion to wear a light dress, and though we would not advocate the nudity of the original players, the Indians, we think the less and lighter the dress the better."

W. G. Beers, the game's leading historian and a lyrical one, at that, was moved to write of the excitement engendered by lacrosse: "Gouty old gentlemen forget their big toes in the excitement of watching a struggle for the ball; the faces of crusty bachelors soften into the old smiles of their youth. Prudes forget their primness, snobs their propriety, old women fearlessly expose themselves to dismantling, young ladies to the demolishment of crinoline and waterfall, dogs will rush frantically over the field and often the ball, and an epidemic of laughter seizes the crowd at the ridiculous incidents and misfortunes of unlucky men."

Modern purists are apt to insist that there are no games in the middle of the 1960s that exude a full-blooded Canadian flavour, including even curling and hockey. They will claim that curling is not much different from the original game imported from Scotland, simply that Canadian refinements have embellished the early product. They will point to the American influence on hockey, too, the concessions to the U.S. bloodlust in the loose interpretation of rules that condone fights and rough play. The charge does not survive scrutiny, however; games were as tough and blood flowed even more freely in the years preceding the game's invasion of the large U.S. centres in the 1920s. Jack Adams, Detroit's coach and general manager for thirty-odd years, recalls a game in the pre-American era between the Toronto Arenas, for whom he played, and the Montreal Wanderers, who carved him up so freely that he came out looking like the loser of a sabre duel at Stuttgart. When the game ended he was wheeled to the Montreal General Hospital where his sister was a nurse, and, indeed, it was she who admitted him. He was so battered and bloodied, however, that she didn't recognize him until he registered at the admitting desk.

"It wasn't an unusually tough game," Adams said airily years later. "When you got cut in those days you

Some sports curiosities stay, and some go. Ladies still bowl, but now they do it one-handed. Lacrosse on skates, alas, is gone – but hockey borrowed many terms and rules from this – *game*?

The big game of '84: New York vs. Montreal Shamrocks.

skated to the boards, where the trainer sloshed off the blood with a sponge he kept in a water bucket and patched you up with a slice of adhesive tape. That night, most of my tape must have sweated off."

But there is, undeniably, a great American influence on the majority of our games. It is ironic, of course, that this is particularly true of Canadian football. Americans coach and play the key positions, and the rules creep inexorably to fit the American pattern. Even the scoring was altered in the late 1950s to make the game less confusing to American recruits and potential television viewers, the five-point touchdown

being switched to the American six. The irony of these conformities is that it was Canada that introduced the game to the United States in the first place. The introduction took place on May 15, 1874, at Cambridge, Massachusetts, the site of Harvard University. The Harvard soccer team had invited the rugby team from McGill University to play two games, one under Harvard's rules and one under McGill's. The Harvards were so entranced by some aspects of rugger – running with an egg-shaped ball, tackling the runner and the revolutionary drop-kick – that they took up the game and passed along the rules to Yale and

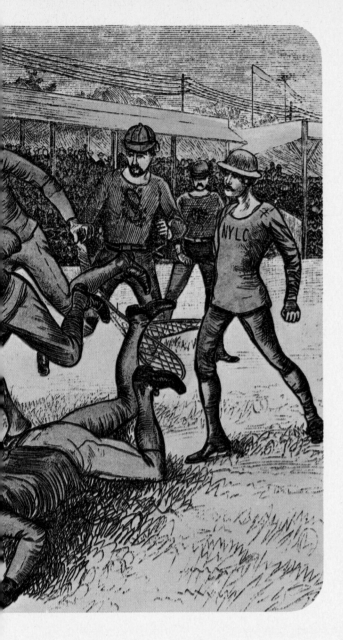

was hired – in 1927 – by Rutgers University to join the coaching staff. He stayed for two years, after a remarkable career as a prep-school star at Bellafonte Academy near Pittsburgh, where he played under the renowned coach, Carl Snavely. Snavely, in a letter to a Toronto columnist in 1940, said that Conacher "was probably the greatest athlete that I have ever coached in football or in any other form of athletics, and it has been my good fortune to have on my teams some of the greatest football players who ever played American football, All-Americans who will be remembered for generations because of their outstanding performances."

Lamenting that Conacher had decided to play professional hockey instead of continuing in football, Snavely, who had later coached at Pittsburgh and Cornell, added, "I don't believe I have ever had a fullback who was a better runner in an open field, or who was a better punter, or who so fully possessed all of the qualities of speed, skill, dexterity, aggressiveness, self-control and the various attributes that are required for superiority in the American game of football. He was far superior to many boys on the same team who later won All-American honours in several universities."

Conacher turned to hockey because in the 1920s, when he was at his peak, it was the only Canadian game at which a man could make a living. In 1950 he was voted, by a national poll of sportswriters, the greatest athlete in Canada of the half-century. In the 1940s there emerged another many faceted paragon, Gordon Howe, who, had he not turned to hockey, very likely would have paralleled Conacher's all-round proficiency. Both excelled in any game they turned to and, between them, they probably best represent the essence of all the ingredients of greatness described in this volume.

They shared one more – and this one was characteristic of Canada's first hundred years of sport, though by no means a solely Canadian characteristic. Conacher and Howe both emerged from big, hardworking families that raised big, self-reliant youngsters, families that lived and grew up by the sweat of their brows and earned their own earthy kind of distinction, starting from scratch in the face of searing competition in many phases of life. Howe was born fifth in a family of nine that grew up on the farmlands near Floral, Saskatchewan; Conacher was the oldest of ten who lived on the fringes of poverty in downtown Toronto. Both of them used sports as a vehicle of escape from a binding environment, and if one were to point to a single Canadian and say, "Look, there, *that's* what's Canadian about Canadian sports; there it is," one could do no better than to identify the ingredients that constituted Gordon Howe or Lionel Conacher.

But we have others with special ingredients, too, we Canadians, as you will see in the body of this book.

Princeton. The first American game followed five months later, when Harvard played Yale.

A further ironic twist is the idea that Canada invented the practice of importing foreign stars to show the natives how football should really be played. It is true that the Calgary Tigers brought a hulk named Gerry Seiberling from Drake University to play in Calgary in 1929, that Curt Shave went to Regina from the University of North Dakota in 1931 and Warren Stevens to the Montreal Winged Wheelers from Syracuse University in the same year. But before any of these importations, Lionel Conacher, of Toronto,

When this picture was taken, in the '20s, Conacher was a *real* triple threat. Once he played an afternoon lacrosse game, a twilight baseball game, and football at night.

Athlete of the century

Lionel Conacher's name led all the rest on every ballot but three when the Canadian Centennial Library asked leading sports editors across the country to name the outstanding athlete of Canada's century. There is no novelty in this: in the Sports Hall of Fame at the CNE, Conacher has long been given pride of place as the all-round athlete who out-played and outfought *everybody*. Partly this was because of his time and place. The Big Train shoved and scrambled out of Toronto's semi-slums in an era when muscular youngsters tried their hands at every sport there was. In the late 1920s the day of the athletic specialist had not yet arrived, but this was not Conacher's fault, and in his violent way he did magnificently everything he tried. He was Grey Cup scoring champion, captain of Stanley Cup teams, star of championship lacrosse and baseball teams, champion boxer, champion wrestler. He was least skillful on the ice, but that was where the money was. So The Big Train went out and became the most awkward *all-star* defenseman in the history of the NHL.

Still playing hard at 57, he hit (*right*) a triple in MPs vs. Press Gallery softball game. Running the bases, going all out, he died.

Into his 50s he went on playing benefit games with old-time NHL players (*at left,* the great goalie Roy Worters). In NHL, Conacher played for Pittsburgh, Chicago, Montreal.

Tom Longboat, here winning the Boston Marathon in 1907, was often called "the greatest distance runner of them all." A Six Nations Indian, he beat the best marathoners of his day here and in Europe, then turned professional and broke the world record for 15 miles.

ENDURANCE

When they've given it all they've got, the great ones give it more.

In the 1920s and early 1930s, the definitive word in sports was endurance. Ernst Vierkoetter, The Black Shark, could swim forever. This made him the darling of the mobs who descended on Lake Ontario's waterfront for the annual Wrigley Swim, an exhausting marathon that highlighted the CNE.

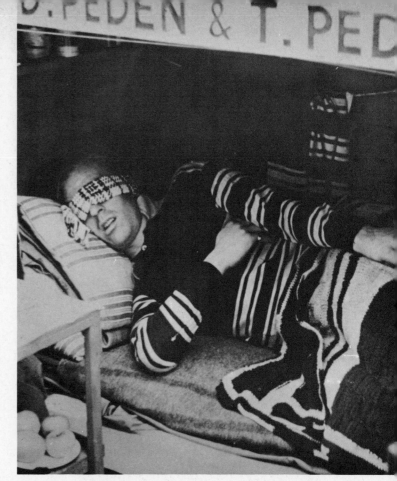

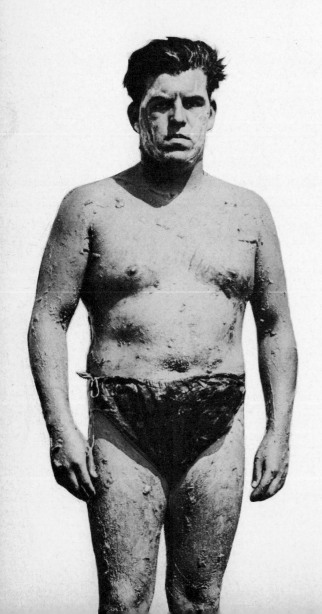

Not all of the long-lasting endurance heroes were water-logged. Six-day bike riders constantly went no place in an endless circle, pausing only to catnap (like Torchy Peden, *above*) in tiny huts at trackside, When Peden was awake, *right above*, he was the fastest man on two wheels, and the two-man team of Torchy and his brother Doug became international celebrities in a world that went round and round and knew no daylight.

Royalty, too, was caught up in the craze for endurance

Toronto's George Young gained instant fame at 17 by winning the $25,000 Catalina Island swim in 1927. Young was acclaimed at home but his renown was capricious. Soon an annual cry became a cliché on the shores of Lake Ontario: "They've taken George Young out of the water."

Small and startled, the 112-pound Hamilton marathoner Bill Sherring looked up from under his straw hat and glimpsed royalty in 1906. On the last lap of his marathon victory at Athens that year, Sherring was joined by Crown Prince Constantine, who finished second.

Smirle Lawson (with ball) was the first Canadian athlete to earn the title Big Train. He always played 60 minutes — above, for U. of T. against McGill in first Grey Cup game, 1907.

Why do goalies get ulcers? Look at Glenn Hall, Chicago's Mr. Goalie, in this 1962 photo. Hall holds the NHL record for games played by a goalkeeper — but he's human, too.

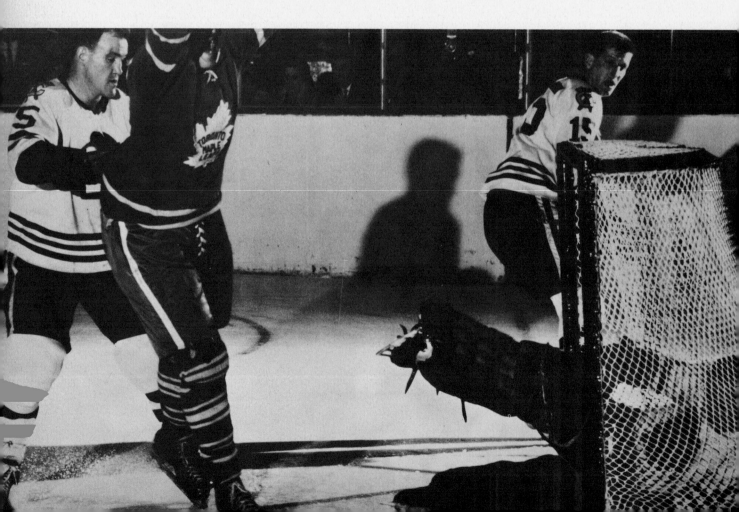

Sam Langford was a light-heavyweight from Nova Scotia who met the world's best heavyweights in the first quarter of this century and defeated most of them. Long after the age when most athletes have become spectators, Langford was still a principal in some of the longest, most brutal prize fights in ring history.

Sam Langford never did learn to quit fighting

Langford had unusually long arms and a barrel chest; sports writers of his day liked to say he had an ape's shape. They also decided, in many cases, that he was "the greatest fighter, pound for pound, who ever lived." Many modern experts agree. Langford lived out his days in a furnished room in Boston, still fighting vicariously — but they were other men's fights, heard on radio. Langford himself was almost blind and almost crippled, as his legacy from the ring.

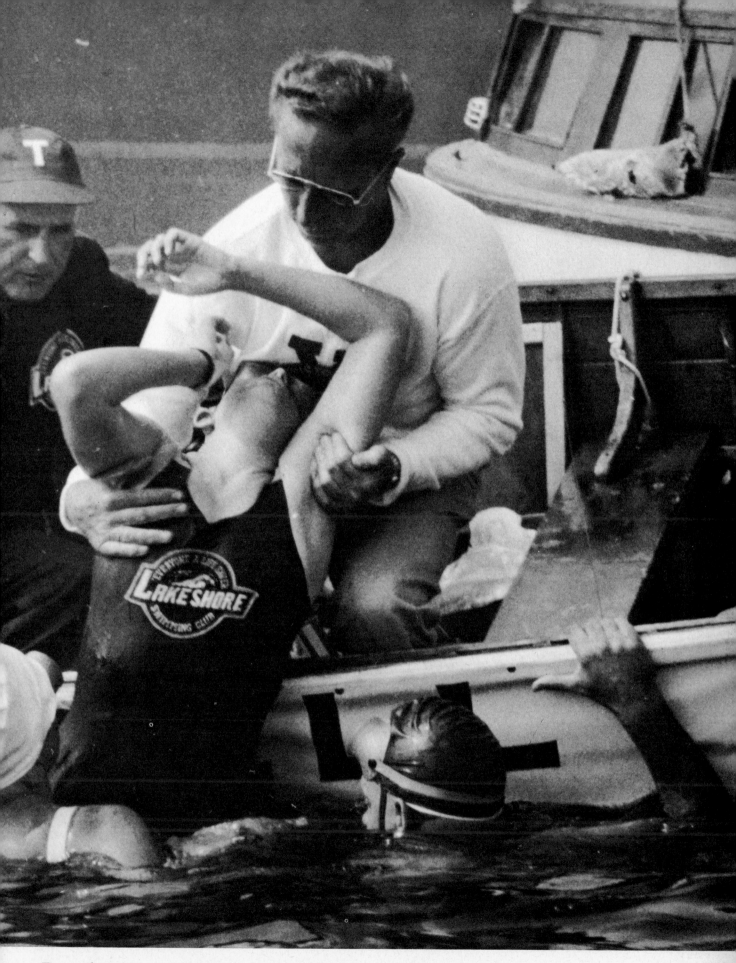

But there is a limit to any athlete's endurance.
Even Marilyn Bell reached it – in the Strait of Juan de Fuca.

MARILYN BELL

The frightening night and the terrible day

Lady athletes are a special case. The tendency among stout-hearted males is to regard them as a contradiction in terms, and to ignore them. This has never been easy. The most exciting performance by a Canadian athlete at the 1960 Winter Olympics was a lady's — Ann Heggtveit, of Ottawa, won Canada's first gold medal in skiing. Before her, Ethel Catherwood, Saskatoon, had leaped higher than any other woman in the world at the 1928 Olympics. That was the year when Canada's four-girl team of sprinters won a gold medal in the 400-metre relay. Later on, Barbara Ann Scott became a three-word synonym for figure-skating, and still later little Marlene Stewart defeated the world's best women golfers. But there was one lady athlete who had a season of glory so intense that no one, male or female, could ignore her altogether. She was Marilyn Bell, sixteen years old the night she swam across Lake Ontario, in September of 1954.

Marilyn looked like somebody's baby-sitter, blue-eyed and honey-haired, shy and soft of speech. Yet she endured a more punishing test than any that several generations of male stoics had been able to withstand before her. At the turn of the century, boxing bouts that lasted thirty and forty rounds were not uncommon, and hockey and lacrosse players were almost all sixty-minute men. In the 1930s, again, endurance was once more a prime athletic quality. In some foot races in the '30s the contestants eventually stopped running and started walking in the manner of somnambulists with hives; one of the characteristic spectacles of the era was a coast-to-coast walkathon called the Bunion Derby.

Long-distance swimming and six-day bike races and even marathon flagpole sitting flourished for a decade, and then they died.

More and more, sport came to stress speed and downgrade stamina, as the nature of the games changed and sixty-minute men became extinct. Endurance for its own sake had been long out of style by the time Marilyn Bell, a solemn, freckle-faced schoolgirl of five-feet-two and 119 pounds, won international acclaim for the most remarkable feat of endurance in the history of Canadian sport.

The ordeal of Marilyn Bell began in the flat black waters of Lake Ontario fifty-three minutes before midnight on September 8, 1954. Ahead of her lay perhaps thirty miles of numbing cold, semi-consciousness and self-denying courage. And, of course, ahead of her lay a lasting achievement as well.

It is the achievement that surmounts the years; forgotten except by the girl herself, and perhaps by the handful of people in a few boats who spent twenty hours and fifty-nine minutes in her wake, are the frightening night and the terrible day in the water.

The swim traversed the lake from Youngstown, New York, at the mouth of the Niagara River, to the Canadian National Exhibition breakwater at Toronto. The course lay across twenty-one miles of water. In the shifting winds that turned the lake from calm to choppy to heavily swelled and back again, the girl in the water was blown many uncharted miles from a direct course, perhaps as many as ten, and although there were at least four times when it seemed she could not possibly survive another stroke, she persevered one way and another and beat the ungiving waters.

The swim began as a lure for the c.n.e. It involved Florence Chadwick, a thirty-four-year-old marathon swimmer from California, who was offered twenty-five hundred dollars by the c.n.e. to tackle the lake and seventy-five hundred more if she beat it. Uninvited, Marilyn and Winnie Roach Leuszler, a girl of twenty-eight from St. Thomas, Ontario, challenged Miss Chadwick. The Toronto *Telegram*, co-sponsor with the c.n.e. of the Chadwick promotion, refused to recognize the challenge, and a nice little newspaper war was in the making. It burgeoned into a front-page story, with six-inch banner headlines, when the Toronto *Star* underwrote the challengers' expenses, and rented boats to accompany them across the lake.

At this moment, very little was known of Marilyn Bell except within the shallow confines of marathon swimming, a phenomenon that briefly raised its soggy head each July at Atlantic City and each September at Toronto's Exhibition. The name of Marilyn Bell had flickered across the sports pages in July, 1954, when she was seventh at Atlantic City and the first female to finish a twenty-six-mile race open to both sexes.

Still, in September, officials of the c.n.e. pleaded with the *Star* to withdraw the support it had offered Marilyn. As the c.n.e. sports director, George Duthie, put it: "That lake is no place for a youngster." The *Star* refused, presumably because of the battle its headline writers were now waging against the *Telegram*. "She sold more newspapers than any news event since the war," a *Star* circulation man said after the swim, noting that both papers sold thirty thousand

more copies than usual on the day of the swim and the day after it.

Because of Marilyn's youth and the comparative obscurity of marathon swimming, neither the newspapers nor the c.n.e. officials were aware that Marilyn had been an accomplished swimmer for at least six years. She was born in Toronto on October 19, 1937, and her father, a spare, retiring clerk-accountant for a food chain, taught her to swim when she was four. Six years later he bought her a season ticket to an outdoor pay-as-you-swim pool. By the next summer Marilyn had won her first swimming award, a medal for stroking a mile in forty-two minutes. The coach at the pool, Alex Duff, asked her to join a group of junior swimmers called the Dolphinettes, who put on demonstrations to raise money for the Community Chest. Through Duff, Marilyn met Gus Ryder, a tough-minded, white-haired swimming coach who ran classes at the Lakeshore Memorial Pool. Ryder invited her to join his swimming club which, between meets, taught crippled children to swim.

"She was the most charming kid, thoughtful and eager," Ryder later recalled. "She had a sort of deep well, a kind of reservoir, and a tremendous loyalty."

When Marilyn was thirteen she began giving swimming lessons to the crippled children. At fourteen she was a professional instructor.

This was the background, then, of young Marilyn Bell when she drove to Youngstown, New York, with Ryder and Joan Cooke, a blond, vibrant friend who was also an instructor at Ryder's Lakeshore Memorial Pool. Bad weather delayed the swim for two days during which Marilyn, her parents, Ryder and some

A dazed automaton, Marilyn Bell neared shore and found a frenzied city waiting to greet her.
Two days earlier, she had been an unknown schoolgirl.

Star reporters and photographers moved aboard *Mona IV*, a boat chartered by the *Star*. Marilyn dozed and read, or left the boat for long walks. She said then that two things concerned her: a gnawing distaste for swimming in the dark, and a loathing of eels and lampreys fastening to her skin. As it turned out, her apprehensions were fully realized.

At a little after nine on the night of September eighth a rainstorm broke over Youngstown. Ninety minutes later it passed, leaving the lake mirror calm. Word reached the *Mona IV* that Florence Chadwick was preparing to take off. Then, as the American swimmer moved out through the black water, Marilyn threw off her dark red blanket, kissed her parents, walked to the edge of the lawn in front of the U.S. Coast Guard building, and plunged off the retaining wall. It was seven minutes past eleven.

Ahead, in the twenty-four-foot lifeboat *Mipepa*, Gus Ryder shone a flashlight to guide her. In these early moments Marilyn refused to let her mind dwell on the dark mystery around her. She recalled that in the water at Atlantic City she had hummed *O Canada* and *The Happy Wanderer*. For now, she confined her thoughts to overtaking Miss Chadwick. After a few hours, a sucking sensation prickled high on her thigh — a lamprey. Shuddering, but forcing herself to be calm, she knocked it away with her fist. Three more times before dawn eels, sucking, attached themselves to her flesh. Each time she knocked them away, without hysteria.

Marilyn caught Florence Chadwick three miles out, and drummed ahead, crawling as purposefully as a fireman skinning up a ladder. Far back, Winnie Roach Leuszler had become separated from her pilot boat; she climbed aboard a press launch, returned to Youngstown, removed her grease, and went to bed. She slept until six in the morning, then plunged into the lake again. Her second attempt was doomed; near nightfall, still nine miles from the Canadian side, she was hauled from the water like an exhausted sailfish, sobbing and only half conscious.

The wind rose towards dawn, building foam-flecked waves twelve feet high. They made Miss Chadwick ill, but she stifled her nausea for another hour. Then, exhausted and half-drowned, she too was lifted from the water. She had managed twelve miles.

Now Marilyn was facing her own crises, treading water glassy-eyed. Ryder, impassive, passed the bewildered girl a cup of corn syrup on the end of a long stick. She took it and stared vaguely as it spilled into the tossing water. Ryder extended another cup. She sipped it, listless as a child with fever, then rolled over and began the endless, staggered rhythm of her stroke.

Full light showed her haggard and gaunt. Pain probed her arms and legs, her stomach throbbed. Her breathing and her stroke had lost their co-ordination, and she gulped unwanted water from the lake. She began to cry. Ryder extended liniment on the stick for her dragging legs. She slowly sank her head, forced her legs above the surface, and rubbed on the liniment. Then she plodded on.

Ryder used Miss Chadwick's capitulation as a psychological device. At ten-thirty, as Marilyn faltered again, he scrawled on a blackboard, FLO IS OUT. At noon he wrote, DON'T LET THE CRIPPLED KIDS DOWN. By early afternoon, she was dozing. She had not been to bed now for thirty hours. The Toronto Harbour Commissioners, fearing she might drown, dispatched two lifeboats to flank her. In mid-afternoon Ryder summoned Joan Cooke, who swam fully clothed to the *Mipepa* from a nearby launch.

At five in the afternoon, with Marilyn seemingly lifeless, Ryder sent Miss Cooke into the water. In pants and a bra, she swam alongside and shrilly wakened her wallowing friend. Then she pulled away in a brisk crawl and Marilyn, woodenly revived but groggy, gave chase.

The wind died, and now crosscurrents underwater played tricks with her course. For every few hundred yards she swam, she drifted half that many from her true line. After an hour and a half of this, she wearily stilled her arms and turned her pale, pathetic face to the pilot boat. Streaks of oil and dirt creased her cheeks, broken by the crooked paths of tears. Her father, aboard the *Mona IV*, ordered her out. Ryder gave no hint he had heard; he raised his blackboard — IF YOU QUIT I QUIT.

The words registered dully. She drew a long breath, her legs and arms responded to some deep and distant message, and the grim employment began anew . . . stroke . . . stroke . . . stroke. Some well of reserve, some channel of reflex kindled her. She never faltered again. She stopped once, to take the last of the syrup and some pablum. Then, a water-logged automaton, she crawled towards the distant, glittering fair grounds.

In the gathering dusk ahead, tens of thousands of people, caught up by the breathless newscasts and the bizarre headlines, welcomed the approach of Marilyn's white cap, a tiny periscope inching to the breakwater. During her hours in the black water she had become a talisman of courage for the city and for people far beyond it. The hope and the tension were contagious — as the sun sank, her partisans clogged every approach to the shoreline she was straining toward, and for these few hours, elsewhere in Canada, radio was once again the supreme bringer of the word. At six minutes past eight her left hand touched the concrete wall. She hung there a moment, gasping for air, and then Ryder and a reporter pulled her into the *Mipepa*. Dazed and disconnected as a punch-drunk fighter, she struggled against their hands, reflexively resisting help. Indeed, it wasn't until Joan Cooke leaped into an ambulance beside her, crying, "Oh, Marilyn, you did it! You did it!" that she knew all the lake was behind her.

TRENT FRAYNE

NERVE

Bob Hayward, the quiet man in the powerful boat above, had it to the ultimate degree. When the calculated risk he took so often was once calculated wrong, he lost his life. Many of Canada's top athletes in other fields have had it too — that icy confidence that allows them to lay their lives on the line in the name of sport.

Ted Hogan held most of the Canadian records for driving a stock car fast (and dangerously) when this picture was taken early in 1960. Before the year was out Hogan was dead. Cars weren't fast enough for him; he was killed flying a light plane.

Blasting into a curve with a surgeon's calm and a gambler's prayer

Vic Emery used to fly torpedo bombers, touching them down, when his day's work was done, on the pitching deck of an aircraft carrier. Back in civilian life, Canada's traditional winter sports must have looked too dull to him, too safe. He turned to one of the world's most dangerous forms of racing — bobsledding — even though when Emery and a group of friends started there were no international-class runs here. By 1964, Emery and his crew had taught themselves enough to scorch the ice, and at the Innsbruck Olympics they surprised the sports world by winning a gold medal for Canada. In 1965, as if to prove their skill and nerves were holding firm, they went back to St. Moritz, Switzerland, and added the world's title. Photo below shows a winning run at St. Moritz.

On August 21, 1961, Bette Singer, a slim,
blond housewife and mother from Cooksville, Ontario,
slipped into the blue Bahaman water and swam down,
down, down, past vision, 307 feet deep, 37 feet
farther than any woman had been under water before.
The perils to her life were enormous. Mrs. Singer,
who had been diving for eight years, knew them
all. "I just wanted to be first," she said.

On July 1, 1962, Peter Ryan, handsome young son
of a resort owner from Mont Tremblant, Quebec,
crashed his Lotus Ford Cosworth in a race near Rheims,
France, suffering multiple fractures and
internal injuries. He died shortly afterward.
Ryan had been one of Canada's top competitive skiers
before giving up skiing to race cars. "At skiing,"
he had once said, "you can only break your leg."

In the Stanley Cup playoffs of 1960, the Detroit Red Wings' Gordie Howe, already emerging as the greatest all-round player hockey has known, roared across the ice to check Toronto's Ted Kennedy. Kennedy stopped short. Howe hit the boards. He crumpled, blood running from his nose and eye. For twenty-four hours his life was in danger. Howe started the next season wearing a helmet *(above)* to shield the injury. Then he discarded it. "It makes me sweat," he said. That year he set an NHL scoring record.

The games that sometimes kill

In May of 1965, Pat Remillard, aged 59, fell from his mount Jiveoli scant yards from the scene of an accident that, only a few years previously, had killed a jockey forty years Remillard's junior. Next day, Remillard rode again.

In December of 1933, Ace Bailey of Toronto was checked by Boston's Eddie Shore. He lay in hospital for days on the edge of death. Months later *(above)*, Bailey shook Shore's hand in public — but his presence was a constant reminder of hockey's built-in dangers.

BOB HAYWARD

The outer edges of skill and luck

Since 1961 the boat has lain in glistening silence in a London, Ontario, marine shop—*Miss Supertest III*, a great, hooded, three-ton rocket whose forty-thousand-dollar engine has roared its last. *Miss Supertest III* had a short life: designed in 1958 and retired three years later, she raced only four times. But no one ever beat her. From 1959 to 1961 she was the fastest hydroplane in the world, three times winner of the Harmsworth trophy, the top challenge trophy for boats of unlimited power.

Miss Supertest III was retired when her driver, Bob Hayward, was killed at the wheel of her older sister-boat, *Miss Supertest II*. Jim Thompson, Hayward's boss and owner of both boats, is a calm, practical graduate of Royal Roads Military College and a man not given to sentimental gestures. Thompson doesn't say *Miss Supertest III* was retired because of Hayward's death—only that the death "accelerated a decision we were going to take anyway; we had been racing long enough, and we were going to get out—maybe the next year. When Bob was killed that was the time to do it." But to anyone who knew Hayward, the silent hull is, inevitably, a personal memorial: a testament to his willingness to test the outer edges of power and skill and luck.

It was the luck that killed him. It must have been, though even those who saw the accident will never know precisely how the luck went wrong. The art of piloting a hydroplane lies principally in taking the curves, and Hayward was a master. The trick is in anticipating the curve. The driver begins turning his rudder while he is still on the straightaway a couple of hundred feet away. At the same time, he decelerates. By the time he hits the turn he is skidding, broadsiding, awaiting the exact second to slam back toward top speed. On September 10, 1961, Hayward was driving *Miss Supertest II* in the Silver Cup regatta at Detroit—*Miss Supertest III* was reserved for the more important Harmsworth races. It was the start of the second heat. *Miss Supertest* was third across the line in the moving start, behind *Century 21*, driven by Bill Muncey, and *Miss U.S. I*, driven by John Wilson. Hayward was pouring on the power, trying to get into position to slip into the lead at the turn. Suddenly it was evident to everyone that the boat was going too fast—that it was out of control. Wilson later described his own view of the accident: "We went into the turn at a hundred and forty and we'd slowed down to a hundred and thirty-five when I saw *Miss Supertest* for the first time. Her right side actually passed right over me as she went by. She was airborne, and doing thirty or forty miles an hour faster than we were. I ducked down in my cockpit. I saw Hayward fighting to get control."

Miss Supertest bounced brutally from side to side in the rough water, still out of control. Then she flipped over, crashing Hayward into the waves and wrenching him back as she came to rest right side up. Hayward's neck was broken. The first rescue boat to reach the hull found him lying across the torn stabilizers at the stern, his life jacket torn away. The entire top of the boat had been ripped off.

On September 14, Hayward was buried in his home village of Embro, in the rolling farm country of western Ontario. Loudspeakers were set up outside Knox Presbyterian Church so that the overflow crowd, including most of the best-known names in international powerboat racing, could hear the service. Hayward was thirty-three when he was killed.

Among men who lay their lives on the line in the name of sport, nerve shows in different ways. In some cases, perhaps the best known ones, it comes out as flamboyance. Peter Ryan, a rich man's son from Mont Tremblant, Quebec, was as good a skiing prospect as Canada has ever had, but he gave up skiing for autoracing because, as he once told a reporter, "at skiing you can only break your leg." Ryan was killed in Europe, in the season of his first success with the cars. Such men seem driven, like war-lovers or compulsive gamblers. Their courage somehow doesn't fit into the normal spectrum of human values.

Other men seem to have nerve the way a good golfer has timing. It is simply part of their make-up.

They may be aware that death is a possible outcome of competition, but they are not hypnotized by its presence. Their nerve is maximum, but it is human too. They pursue their sports in spite of the risk, not because of it, and perhaps in the truest sense that makes them the bravest athletes of all.

Bob Hayward was one of these. The last word anyone would have applied to him was flamboyance. In most gatherings of athletes, or of chicken-farmers (which he also was), he was remarkable only for being inconspicuous. He was quiet, diffident, polite, friendly. He was stocky, even pudgy, with brown eyes and a slow, warm smile. His hands were square and stubby, the hands of a mechanic. He knew motors, and for every hour he spent behind the wheel of one of the Supertest speedboats he spent a hundred more tinkering with the design and the tuning. "He can feel an engine," Vic Leghorn, the mechanic who served as crew chief of the Supertest team, once said of him. "He knows exactly what it can do."

For a world champion, Hayward received little honour at home. In 1960, the year he won the Harmsworth for the second time, Belgium gave him a gold medal. But he was seventh in the Canadian Press vote for athlete of the year, far behind Ron Stewart, the football player, and hockey's Bobby Hull. Still, he was occasionally asked to speak at banquets, and the Supertest Corporation tried to keep him in the public eye. As he gained some experience at appearing in front of people, he learned to master his innate shyness. The quality he projected most strongly was capability. His speech was as sure as it was slow. There was a control about everything he did, from adjusting a bushing to addressing a Kiwanis Club. He never undertook anything until he knew how it ought to be done; then he did it that way. The excitement he got from racing hydroplanes was the excitement of control, not of risk. He knew exactly what he was doing when he was at the wheel, and – until his luck turned on the Detroit River – exactly what he *could* do.

Hayward was born in Embro in 1928 and like many Ontario farm boys he took to motors early. Coincidentally, he raced outboards as a boy, but when he was old enough to get a driver's license he turned to cars. He built a dragster – a stock car designed for speed – when he was still in his teens, and raced it on the dust tracks of the farm country. It was once clocked at 123 miles an hour. Even after Hayward had won three Harmsworths, he liked to recall that he had set the unofficial track record for one lap at Nilestown, Ontario. With a brother, Hayward worked a chicken farm at Embro and started in the trucking business, until, in 1947, Jim Thompson asked him to join Thompson's racing crew to help tune *Miss Supertest II* for a race.

Thompson, president of the Supertest Petroleum Corporation, had until then done most of the driving himself, with moderate success. Hayward began test-driving *Miss Supertest II*, and soon worked up to pilot. In his first year he set a world speed record for propeller boats: 184 miles an hour. In 1958 Thompson decided to make a bid for the Harmsworth Trophy – which no Canadian had ever won – and he started to work on the plans for *Miss Supertest III*.

The simplest way to describe a hydroplane is to say it rides on the water like an inverted saucer with the ends chipped out. At high speed it rides, in fact, on a cushion of air. The top speed of *Miss Supertest III* was never determined – it would have been well over 180 miles an hour. At, say, 160, the only parts touching the water were half the propeller, fourteen inches of rudder and a strip the length of a man's hand of each forward sponson (the downturned lips of the saucer). The reason *Miss Supertest III* was never taken to her top speed is that a hydroplane driven too fast simply takes off. Hayward once spoke of seeing a hydroplane rise from the end of a swell and do a complete loop-the-loop in the air.

The effort required to pilot one of these boats is enormous. "The forty-five miles of a Harmsworth race," Hayward once said, "takes just as much out of me as running hard for twenty-five minutes." The higher the speed the harder a hydroplane is to steer. To save drag, *Miss Supertest III*'s thirteen-inch rudder was set half way out of the water. Her propeller was driven by a two-thousand-horsepower Rolls-Royce Griffon engine; the blades sliced into the waves eleven thousand times a minute. The driver needed great strength at the wheel just to keep the propeller's force from "walking" the boat sideways.

From 1958 on, Hayward and his crew chief, Leghorn, a wiry Englishman, worked full time on the boat. They stripped and inspected the hull, and took apart most of the engine, at least six times a year. Under Thompson's guidance, they were constantly modifying their boat. They knew exactly how long every part would last, and changed every item before it wore out The bushing in the wheel case, as an example, was replaced after every ninety minutes of running time.

By the racing season of 1959, *Miss Supertest III* was ready. As a tune-up, the crew entered and won the Detroit Memorial on the river where Hayward was to be killed only two years later.

The Detroit River was also the scene of the Harmsworth races that year. They were held during three days in late August – one race each day of fifteen laps around a three-mile triangular course. Hayward's opponent was the American champion, *Maverick*, driven by Bill Stead. *Miss Supertest III*, at three tons, weighed a thousand pounds more than *Maverick*; she was heavier than nearly all the U.S. boats of her day (though lighter than *Miss Supertest II*). The two boats were closely matched in speed, though *Miss Supertest* seemed to have a slight edge. The race was as much a test of drivers as of boats. Hayward won the first day's race handily, but during the second he

went into a "hook"—too flat a skid at the turn—on an early lap, and was beaten.

For the final day, Hayward's strategy was to give Stead the inside lane for the moving start. Instead of working for position, he concentrated on timing. His plan worked. *Miss Supertest III*'s orange and white hull flashed across the line almost simultaneously with the sound of the gun. It was the first time in the three days of racing that Hayward had managed to take the lead from the beginning, and he never relinquished it. Before the race, Hayward had expressed some anxiety over the roughness of the water. Choppy water is not as dangerous for hydroplanes as the swells that can send them soaring, but it doesn't make for easy driving either. Once, driving *Miss Supertest II* in the Detroit Memorial, Hayward hit some choppy water at 130 miles an hour. He could see a black stripe in the wall of water that went up as the nose dipped, and he sensed something wrong with the hull. He slowed down, and lost the race. Afterward he found a hole in the cherry-plywood hull big enough to pass a loaf of bread through.

One turn around the Harmsworth course that August afternoon in 1959, though, convinced Hayward the water was smooth enough for a maximum run. "I really opened her up," he told a reporter from the Toronto *Star* after the race. "I must have been hitting a hundred and seventy on the backstretch." On the second lap he averaged 109.334 miles an hour. "That's the fastest I've had this baby going," Hayward said. It was also a Harmsworth record.

Toward the end of the third lap Hayward got the break that clinched the Harmsworth for Canada.

Stead, trying vainly to catch the flying *Miss Supertest*, put his own boat into a hook. Hayward roared steadily on. Before *Miss Supertest* finished twelve laps, *Maverick* had stopped. But Hayward, concentrating only on the gauges on his dashboard and the stop-watches he kept strapped to the column of his steering wheel, didn't know he was now alone. "I couldn't find *Maverick*," he said later. "For a while I figured Bill had put on a spurt and was riding just behind me. So I really gave her the gun. All the way down the backstretch and into the turn I still couldn't find *Maverick*. I was beginning to think Stead had stopped. But I still wasn't sure. Then I saw her under the bridge. I knew we had it. I really gunned down the backstretch in the last lap. I figured if the engine conked out then I could just coast in. Then I headed straight for the judges' stand—as close as I could get. I wanted everybody to get a good look at this wonderful boat."

With Hayward's driving, and Leghorn's tinkering, and Thompson's supervision, no one could catch Hayward and his wonderful boat for the next two years. He repeated his Harmsworth victory the next year at Detroit, beating three challengers over a five-mile course. His fastest lap was 126 miles an hour. In 1961, with the Canadian boat now undeniably the hottest racing craft afloat, the Harmsworth moved for the first time ever to Canadian waters—a sheltered bay off Picton, Ontario—and *Miss Supertest III* again won a decisive victory.

Two weeks and five days later, quiet, diffident Bob Hayward was dead, and the hottest racing machine Canada had ever built became a museum piece.

PETER GZOWSKI

Miss Supertest was moving slowly—at about 100 mph—when this picture was taken. Photographer was tied to deck.

Finesse

Every muscle in the supple young body of Petra Burka, Canada's 1965 world champion of figure skating, is under complete control as she spins through a turn and a half in the air. That's finesse — cool style during the heat of action.

In that ballet among sports, gymnastics, Canada has never seen the equal of Ernestine Russell. Ernestine won her first international championship in 1951, when she was 12. At 14 she was our woman athlete of the year. At 16 she won every event in the U.S. championships. Seven times running she was Canadian champion. At her peak she was grace personified, the smoothest athlete of her time.

Three times the most valuable football player in Canada. Eight times an all-star. Seventy-nine touchdowns for the Edmonton Eskimos — including the last-quarter run that beat Montreal 26-25 in 1954 and started Edmonton's three-year hold on the Grey Cup. Jackie Parker, Old Spaghetti Legs, the slickest runner, the cutest quarterback, the player who, in his best years in the west, played football as well and calmly as if he'd written the rules. The player who had everything, but most of all style, finesse.

Some games are all finesse — all concentration and steadiness and glacial calm under stress. The best example of all is pool. And the best North American pool player of modern times is George Chenier, a professional who was born in Toronto in 1907. Chenier once ran up a snooker break of 144—missing a perfect game by three, when he dropped one brown ball along with fourteen blacks.

Johnny Coulon's fighting weight was only 116 pounds, but he was a stylish enough boxer to be world's bantamweight champion. He first claimed the title in 1907, and won it officially by knocking out the British champion Jim Kendrick in 1910. He held it till 1914 — perhaps the most polished boxer of his time.

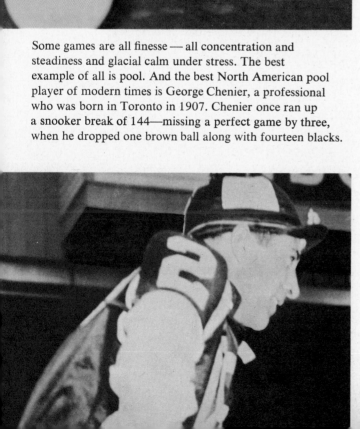

The greater the pressure, the more glacial a champion's calm

George Woolf came out of Cardston, Alberta, to become one of the leading jockeys in North America. In nineteen years of riding, from 1927 to 1946 when he was killed in a racing accident, he won 721 races. Twice he led the continent in money won — but never in wins. He was too dispassionate to ride in minor races just to run up cheap wins — a cool, calm professional whose fans called him The Iceman.

So polished
they shone
against the best

Of the three different Canadian figure-skating pairs who have won world or Olympic titles — Bowden and Dafoe in the early 1950s; Wagner and Paul later in the same decade; the Jellineks in the 1960s — the smoothest, most finished skaters of all, by common consent, were Barbara Wagner and Robert Paul (right), world champions from 1957 to 1960, Olympic gold medalists in 1960.

Toronto's Tommy Gayford (below, aboard a horse called Pepper Knowes) is one of the world's most polished show-riders, and therefore one of the world's most polished athletes. Three years in a row, Gayford won the high jumping event (puissance) in the U.S. national horse show.

Marlene Stewart Streit has won virtually every important event in world women's golf — the British Amateur, the U.S. Open, even the Australian Women's Championship in 1963. Her most distinctive quality on the course: a calm as cool as her off-course personality is warm and winning.

At the quick, delicate sport of badminton, no Canadian — and scarcely anyone from outside Canada — has ever equalled the record of Jack Purcell, of Guelph, Ontario. Purcell completely dominated all Canadian badminton tournaments until he turned pro in 1931.

Appreciative citizens of Ottawa gave their own
Barbara Ann Scott an automobile when she
returned from winning Canada's first Olympic
figure-skating gold medal in 1948. Olympic
officials objected. Then, in a gesture as graceful
as any she made on ice, Barbara Ann gave it back.

The smoothest things on ice since bonded stock

Curlers who came after him opened the game
up, and, with their knockout tactics, made it
almost as much a contest of strength as of
skill. But Ken Watson, the first of the great
Canadian curling champions (he skipped rinks
from Manitoba to the Macdonald Brier Tankard
in 1936, 1942 and 1949), was all finesse
and control, a wise and efficient master craftsman.

Frustrated opposing hockey players, like
the two Detroit Red Wings sandwiching him at
left, agreed that no defenseman in hockey played
with more finesse than Montreal's (and later
New York's) Doug Harvey, seven times winner
of the NHL's most valuable defenseman award.
Never a spectacular skater, and never even
a punishing body-checker, Harvey used skill
alone to become the defensive backbone of
the successful Canadien teams of the 1950s.

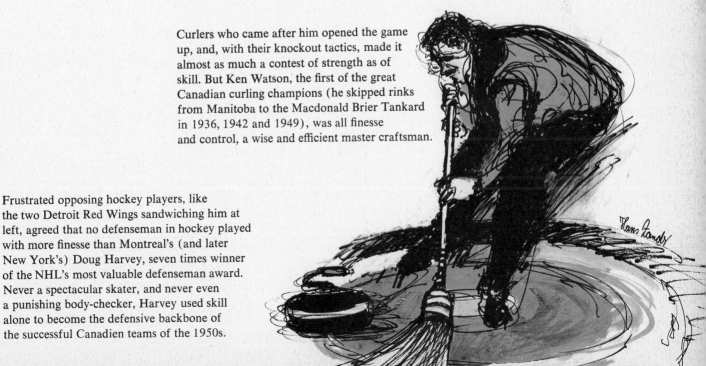

SANDY SOMERVILLE

As smooth as a summer sky

In the great golfing boom that has swept this continent since World War II, golf and golfers have attracted some curious adjectives. A favourite word of golf writers, for instance, is "courageous"—as if it takes courage to hit a little white ball. One American magazine of the 1960s has even published an article called "Golf Is A Violent Game."

But the true essence of golf is finesse—finesse and style and a cool, nerveless resistance to pressure. No Canadian has ever shown more golfing finesse than Sandy Somerville. Somerville won the U.S. National Amateur championship in 1932. He is the only Canadian who ever has. The tournament he won was among the tensest and best-played in the Amateur's history. Somerville played nearly a hundred and eighty holes in six days: two qualifying rounds of eighteen holes; two eighteen-hole elimination matches; and three more of thirty-six holes. Through them all, he scarcely made a mistake. His game was as smooth as a summer sky. He did not out-drive the long hitters, and he did not match the streaks of the hot-and-cold putters; he simply outplayed everyone else. Of the hundred and thirty-six men who started he was the best, the smartest, the steadiest when it counted. On one round he set a competitive course record. But his game was more consistent than brilliant. His victory was a triumph of steady excellence—a true golfer's triumph, a triumph of finesse.

The fact of Somerville's victory was as spectacular and surprising as his play was unruffled—the fact that a golfer from Canada, of all the countries in the world that are cold and unfriendly to golf, could beat the best amateurs in America. No foreigner had been able to win the U.S. Amateur since Harold Hilton of Great Britain in 1911, and in the twenty-one years since Hilton's victory the beginnings of the great boom had brought about a remarkable upsurge in both the quantity and quality of American golf. Earlier in the summer of 1932, a team of U.S. amateurs had beaten Britain in Walker Cup play by the humiliating score of eight to one. No Canadian had done well in the U.S. amateur since George S. Lyon was beaten in the

This is the U.S. National Amateur championship of 1932.

finals of 1906. Lyon had won the Olympic golf championship in 1904, but by 1932 he had been relegated to the status of "grand old man of Canadian golf." Few golf fans could imagine another Canadian ever matching his success.

Somerville, at twenty-nine, was the grand young

The finalists are holing out on the tenth. Somerville is putting. He is the underdog—but today he is unbeatable.

man. The skills he put into golf were a distillation of his abilities at a variety of sports. Sandy—properly C. Ross—Somerville was one of the most remarkable athletes of his day, perhaps the most remarkable amateur athlete Canada has ever produced. He was the son of a well-to-do family from London, Ontario.

His father, a bearded, frock-coated Edwardian gentleman who manufactured Opeechee Chewing Gum, sent young Sandy at the age of ten to Ridley College, an Anglican boys' private school in St. Catharines. Ridley was even then a school with a long tradition of success at sports, but it had seen few boys as gifted and dedicated as the lean young Somerville, and it has seen few since. In the lower school, where he was track and field champion, Somerville attracted attention with his natural ability at cricket, which substitutes for baseball at Ontario's Little Big Four schools. In the upper school, he set records at cricket that have not yet been broken. In one game as a schoolboy he scored two hundred and twelve runs not out – the second highest score ever achieved by a Canadian, equivalent to hitting about five grand slam home runs in one game. Yet as a bowler he allowed the batsmen he faced an average of a shade more than four runs each. His accomplishments at football and hockey were nearly as spectacular. At the University of Toronto, Somerville was a brilliant halfback; he once kicked six field goals in a single game. He was equally good as a hockey centre. Conn Smythe, then a budding entrepreneur of sports, once described Somerville in action as having "a rear end like a tame bee." In another age, or coming from a different background, Somerville would undoubtedly have been a hero of professional sports. After college he led the 12th Battery hockey team from London to an Ontario championship, and he led a cricket team of Canadians on a successful tour of England, where, legend has it with forgivable inaccuracy, he was the first man to hit a six over the stands at Lord's.

But golf was Sandy Somerville's true vocation. The game's demands on polished style, its loneliness, its gentlemanly traditions all seemed to suit the personality of the gentleman's son from London. The first characteristic noticed by anyone who knew Somerville as a young man – or who knows him as a mature one – was his shyness. Tall, slim (over six feet and no more than 170 pounds) and silent – with, as one sportswriter has described it, "a face as long as a maiden's dream" – he let his accomplishments do his talking for him. He was and has continued to be as retiring as he was gifted; a gentleman first and an athlete second, and a golfer all the time.

Somerville first played golf at the age of five, when his family took him on an extended trip to South Carolina. At Ridley he developed his game on a golf course built by a private club on unused school land. By the time he was twenty-one he went as far as the finals of the Canadian Amateur, but was beaten then and the next year. Between 1923 and 1931, though, he won the Canadian championship four times. He was the dominant figure in any Canadian tournament he entered, indisputably the finest amateur golfer in the country.

In his success at home Somerville had many times repulsed American challenges. Henry Roxborough's *Great Days in Canadian Sport* lists ten prominent Americans defeated by Somerville in various Canadian Amateur matches. But away from home his touch seemed to fail. Seven times before 1932 he entered the regional qualifying round for the U.S. National Amateur. Four times he failed to make it into the tournament proper; the other three times he was eliminated early in the match play. In 1931, after winning his fourth Canadian championship, Somerville, in a rare public comment, confided to a reporter that he would never really be satisfied until he had won in the United States. For the next year, the U.S. National Amateur was his constant and single goal.

In the 1930s, as until well after World War II, there was one small but important difference between American and Canadian golf equipment: the American ball was larger and lighter than the ball used in Canada and Britain. The American ball was possibly a little easier to putt with, but it was more susceptible to wind and therefore more difficult to control off the tee or from the fairway. And only the American ball was allowed in American tournaments.

Somerville ignored the lesser Canadian tournaments in 1932. Instead, he started working with the American ball, and waiting for his one big try at the U.S. title. In mid-August, though, he entered the Canadian Amateur at Lambton, in Ontario, to defend his title. To most observers his game looked anything but sharp. He was eighth in the qualifying medal play, and though he won his first matches – including, as usual, one over an American invader, Frank Ryan – he was eliminated in the semi-final by Jack Cameron of Toronto's Mississauga Club. (At that, Somerville did better than a young Vancouver amateur named Stan Leonard.) Cameron subsequently lost the final. Several newspapermen covering the Canadian tournament noted that Somerville's failure had been caused to a considerable degree by his erratic tee-shots. What most of them failed to report was that he had been playing with the larger American ball. He had, in other words, accepted a handicap in the Canadian tournament in order to prepare his game for the American championship. Somerville himself, of course, made no excuses.

The district qualifying rounds for the National were held at Cleveland on the Monday following Somerville's defeat at Lambton, and it was evident that his work with the American ball had paid off. Shooting two masterly sub-par rounds, he led the Cleveland qualifiers by three strokes.

The National Amateur itself was held at Baltimore's famed Five Farms course, in mid-September. Somerville was facing some famous and formidable opposition, most notably the defending champion – and one of the great names in American golfing history – Francis Ouimet. But as the play started most of the danger appeared to come from younger American players. The first two rounds were medal play, serving only to cut the starting field down to the low thirty-two for elimination matches. On Monday, a twenty-year-old named John Fischer, the U.S. college champion, suddenly began playing the best golf of his life. His sixty-nine set a course record. Somerville's seventy-three kept him in contention, but attracted little notice. On Tuesday, Somerville could do no better than a seventy-seven, but his 150 total was good enough to get him into the match play. Fischer qualified with a low score of 142.

There were two afternoon matches on Wednesday for those who survived the cuts, and Somerville won both his. In the first he took the lead at the second hole from John Brawney of San Francisco and went on to win, five holes up with three holes left to play. In the afternoon his game held steady, and he was even par at the end of sixteen holes, beating Jack Westland of Chicago three-and-two. The big story of Wednesday's competition, though, was Ouimet. Ouimet had started his morning round with a scorching first nine of thirty, and had easily taken the measure of his two younger opponents.

On Thursday the play turned to thirty-six-hole matches. Somerville drew Billy Blaney of Boston, and Ouimet drew the hot young Fischer. Somerville's morning round was the best ever shot at Five Farms, a two-under-par sixty-eight, and Blaney was no match for it. The margin was six-and-five. A look at Somerville's morning card shows his steadiness – four birdies, two bogies, the rest pars. While the newspapers were still concentrating on Ouimet, who finally disposed of the upstart Fischer, they were also beginning to take notice of the Canadian.

Somerville's semi-final opponent was Jesse "Siege Gun" Guilford, a former champion and one of the longest drivers in the game. Throughout their match Somerville's tee-shots were twenty and thirty yards short of Guilford's, but he was placing every shot with precision. The man who had lost in the Canadian semi-final because of his erratic driving was now being called the "accurate-driving" Canadian. Somerville was six holes up after the morning round, seven up with six left to play.

Ouimet, meanwhile, had finally fallen, and the man who beat him, Johnny Goodman, was a match for Somerville in determination. Goodman was only twenty-two, but three years before he had beaten Bobby Jones in an early round of the Amateur. In 1932 he had been left off the U.S. Walker Cup team, and he was out for revenge at Baltimore. In the wake of his rise to the final he left not only Ouimet, the Walker Cup captain, but two more of the team's stars as well. He was the giant killer. He was playing so well against Ouimet, someone calculated, that in spite of the walloping Somerville had handed Guilford, Goodman would have been five up on Somerville at the end of thirty holes. Few Americans were worried about their national title leaving the country that year. Four thousand of them turned out to cheer Goodman home on Saturday morning.

From the first tee-shot it was evident the match would be close. Goodman won the first hole, Somerville the second. At the end of nine they were all square. Goodman won the tenth and eleventh, but again Somerville came back to even the match, then go ahead, then slip back to even. On the eighteenth hole Somerville sank the longest putt of the day, a fifty-footer, and, still unsmiling, strode into the clubhouse for lunch, one up. Over one stretch in the morning round Goodman, the U.S. hope, the man who had bested Francis Ouimet just as he had once bested Bobby Jones, had birdied four holes out of five, but the calm serious Canadian had stayed right with him.

In the afternoon Goodman won four holes from Somerville on the first nine. Somerville managed only one winning hole; the young American was now two up. As the two players trudged down the fairway of the tenth hole, the twenty-eighth of the match, the fans began shouting encouragement to Goodman: "Come on, Johnny. Come on, Johnny." But, perhaps bending a little with the pressure, Goodman overshot the green with his second shot and missed a nine-foot putt. Somerville's par lowered the margin to one hole.

At the twenty-ninth Somerville's drive hooked into the rough, and a maple tree ten yards ahead of his lie partly blocked the line of his next shot. Goodman's drive split the fairway. Somerville rejected the easy chip to safety and, with a two-iron, slammed his ball past the tree and to the green, pin high and fifteen feet to one side. This was the shot, under the greatest pressure amateur golf could offer, that many observers consider to have been the turning point of the match. Goodman couldn't answer it. His approach was short, and he took a bogey. Somerville had evened the match.

Goodman hit a trap on the thirtieth hole, and in spite of a fine explosion had to settle for another bogey. Somerville's third straight par gave him a one-hole lead with six holes to play. The next three holes were halved. On the thirty-fourth, Somerville dropped a twelve-foot putt for a birdie and a two-hole lead. The next hole, the seventeenth of the course, was a par three. Goodman missed the green. Somerville drove to within fifteen feet of the pin. Goodman studied his chip shot for anxious minutes, but his ball stopped inches short. Somerville rolled his approach putt dead to the pin, and knocked it in for a par. The half gave him the match and the title, two and one, and Goodman rushed to congratulate him.

Somerville was now the best amateur golfer in America – for that year, anyway, perhaps the best in the world. Surrounded by a crowd of autograph seekers and appreciative fans, including twelve who had travelled from London for the final, he made his way to the clubhouse to accept the twenty-two-thousand-dollar gold trophy. His victory was the biggest sports story of the year in Canada, headlined across the country. That night Sandy Somerville took the New York Central toward home, but he got off at St. Thomas to be driven to London by friends. He couldn't face the prospect of being greeted by a crowd at the station in his home town.

PETER GZOWSKI

When the

Richardsons
set out

to sweep past

rival rinks
the name of

the game *is* **TEAM PLAY**

From two coasts came unlikely championship teams

Rowing was only briefly, and long ago, Canada's top game. Still, the world champions at the Paris Exposition of 1870 — and therefore hailed as "the Paris Crew" — were this four from Saint John, N.B. But the price was desperate; in a race soon after, one man paid a high price for team spirit. See page 94.

Young rowers from the University of British Columbia, coached by Vancouver hotel-owner Frank Read, won startling — and frequent — championships in top-flight competition during the 1950s. UBC crews, eights and fours, were gold and silver medal winners at the Olympics of 1956 and the British Empire Games of 1954. Read was an unpaid and dedicated coach whose oarsmen's record was acclaimed as "unrivalled in the annals of amateur sports in Canada" by UBC's athletic director.

Woman-to-woman teamwork: in the 1924 Olympic Games white-shirted Bobbie Rosenfeld anchored Canada's four-girl relay team. They won a gold medal.

Once, great pattern-passing forward lines abounded, and every NHL team had its production line. Detroit got a record output in the 1950s from Gordie Howe, Sid Abel and Ted Lindsay.

Faces rarely changed on a top line. From the moment the New York Rangers joined the NHL in 1926 until this trio left the scene nearly a decade later, Bun Cook, Frank Boucher and Bill Cook terrorized goaltenders.

The Kraut Line of Boston glowed in the years leading up to World War II — Bobby Bauer, Milt Schmidt, Woody Dumart.

Toronto's Kid Line was most renowned of all — partly because Toronto's announcer, Foster Hewitt, cried out their names coast to coast, Saturday after Saturday, year after year. But the Kid Line of Charlie Conacher, Joe Primeau and Harvey (Busher) Jackson had something else, too: all three could put the puck in the net — Conacher with a booming shot, Primeau, the playmaker, with guile, and Jackson from any angle and with an unmatched flair.

What makes a great line: Three men moving like one

Lacrosse was really Canada's national game in the days before the stars were born, when every player counted to the team. Open fields were the setting, as here at Fort Saskatchewan in 1905, when militiamen from Strathcona played the Edmonton team.

The East's overwhelming domination of football really ended in 1954 when
Oklahoma-schooled coaches took an intricate attacking system called the Split-T
to Edmonton and built a team that won the Grey Cup three years in a row.
Until then, western triumphs had been sporadic. In 1955, the Eskimos used the
masterly timing of the Split-T to confound the Montreal Alouettes and
enchant nearly 40,000 at Vancouver in the first Grey Cup game ever played in the west.

THE EDMONTON GRADS

A quarter-century of utter destruction

The more you think about it the more outlandish it becomes, but the conclusion is inescapable: the greatest Canadian team in a hundred years of sport was the Edmonton Grads, an unwaveringly dedicated assembly of – it has to be said – female basketball players.

Basketball is by no means the definitive game, belonging as it now does to stratospheric goons, and the athletic pits are rarely a place for ladies, involving as they do split lips, coarse language and, worse, underarm odours. Still, the combination of girls and basketball produced a quarter of a century of athletic dominance – from 1915 to 1940 – unmatched by any team playing any game, professional or amateur, man or beast.

The Edmonton Grads, who were not goons and who sweated in a ladylike manner if they sweated at all, beat everybody everywhere. They beat American champions in any city you care to name from San Francisco to New York, and they beat European teams from any city you care to mispronounce from Bobaix to Lille to Rheims to Douai, and from Paris to London to Rome, too. That bunch in Lille they shaded sixty-one to one, and the ladies they caught up with in London must have wandered in from a week in Soho: the Grads' edge there was one hundred to two. In twenty-five years of utter destruction the Grads played 522 games, facing all comers, and won 502. Any arguments?

The Grads played entire seasons without defeat. Once, they compiled a winning streak of 147 successive games; another time it was seventy-eight. During their quarter-century of eminence they lost the provincial championship only once (to the University of Alberta in 1921) and never lost a game in twenty-one western Canada finals. They won the Canadian championship when it was established in 1922 and were never beaten in a national series thereafter, winning twenty-nine games and losing two. They won 138 of 152 games against American opponents. They went to the Olympic Games four times – to Paris in 1924, Amsterdam in 1928, Los Angeles in 1932 and Berlin in 1936 – played twenty-seven games, won twenty-seven, and scored in all 1,863 points. Their opponents ran up 297.

In 1923 a typewriter company made a selfless effort to encourage girls' basketball by establishing a challenge trophy for international competition. In its day the Underwood Challenge Trophy (publicity was a cross the company resigned itself to bear) was just as famous as the Stanley Cup and far more so than the Grey Cup. The first series pitted the Grads against the Cleveland Favorite-Knits, champions of Ohio, and when the teams took the court on the night of June 12, 1923, in the old Edmonton Arena, the Grads looked ridiculous. They wore long woollen stockings, billowing black bloomers with pleats, black middies with sailor collars and thin strands of gold piping, and black-and-gold bands across their foreheads to keep back the flowing hair. By contrast, the Favorite-Knits had either come to play or to mesmerize every man in the house: they wore form-fitting jerseys and short shorts with the letters WORLD'S CHAMPS stamped across them. Then the man blew the whistle and the Grads stopped looking ridiculous. They whipped the svelte visitors in two straight games, and through the best part of the next two decades they withstood forty-nine challengers from every section of the United States.

Of 120 games played for the Underwood Trophy the Grads won 114. In a series against the Chicago Taylor-Trunks the Grads lost the first game by a score of thirty-four to twenty-four, their first loss in seventy-nine games. When they engaged the Taylor-Trunks in the second game on a balmy spring evening early in May, 1930, all previous records for attendance at any sports event in Edmonton were broken. Almost seven thousand spectators jammed into the arena to watch the grim Grads whip the Chicago girls forty to thirteen, easily winning the total-points series.

By then, the Grads were showing a certain chic even before they touched the ball. They wore trim shorts in place of the billowing bloomers, had discarded the long woollen stockings, and their sleeveless knitted jerseys, though modest, at least revealed that girls lurked within, always a point of some uncertainty with the old roomy middies.

The Grads were a reflection of their creator, their one and only coach throughout the quarter-century, John Percy Page, steady, conservative (upper and lower-case; he served two sessions in the Alberta legislature), thorough, solemn, dedicated. On a small scale, J. Percy Page, as he was always called in the newspapers, is a Canadian legend. I say small scale because after the Grads packed up their basketball bras in 1940 he sought the obscurity he had always seemed

54

The Edmonton Grads of 1922, first Canadian champions, were as anonymous as their frightening playsuits.

to covet even at the peak of his team's international renown. He coached for twenty-five years with dignity and propriety, and those were still two of his attributes twenty years later when he was appointed lieutenant-governor of Alberta.

Almost everything about Page was shades of grey, his thick batch of neat wavy hair, his bland nature, his suits, even his coaching philosophy. For all their magnificent record, the Grads were short on panache. They were precision-tuned in endless hours of practice. They had two ninety-minute practice sessions a week and often practised at lunch hours as well. Some of the girls had hoops set up at home. Page was so devoted to his team that he spent one Christmas vacation painting the girls' shower rooms. In twenty-five years he missed only three practices, two of them to campaign for election. He made all the arrangements and bookings for trips, looked after the team's finances, equipment and publicity. His wife Maude went along on most trips as chaperone.

Winning was important but, really, Page wanted the Grads to be ladies first, basketball players second. He was overseer of the company they kept, the places they went. They were not allowed dates on road trips, they could not smoke and, of course, drinking was out of the question. Page expected his players to be quite as dedicated as he was. "You must play basketball, think basketball and dream basketball," he told them. For more than two decades his players called him Mr. Page. Late in the 1930s the Grads of that vintage began to call their by-then white-haired mentor Papa.

The girls obeyed the rules because they considered it an honour to be a Grad; no Grad was ever paid. But there were compensations. The team travelled 125,000 miles – to Europe three times and the United States almost annually – thus providing foreign travel for nearly all the fifty girls who were Grads at one time or another in the slow but inevitable turnover of talent. Edmontonians adored them, called them by name on the street and sought their autographs. Employers cheerfully gave them time off from their jobs. They got numerous gifts from the proud city fathers, watches, bracelets, luggage, sets of silver. One year the city gave Page a Chevrolet coupe. It was his first car; until then, he had ridden a bicycle.

Page coached only the fundamentals of the game, nothing fancy or complicated. A visiting sportswriter once told Page, "The Grads are good, but those plays are so old they've got whiskers on them." Page was unruffled. "I feel if the girls are masters of a dozen plays they can cope with any situation." So Page emphasized ball-handling, shooting, dribbling, passing, physical condition and, above all, teamwork. The fact that fifty girls passed through the Grad system over the years with no major alteration of style illustrates how thoroughly Page was able to integrate each newcomer into his style of play. Each practice was followed by a one-mile run around the perimeter of the basketball court for conditioning, and the team occasionally played men's teams to step up competition.

The Grads were so good that when the man generally acknowledged as basketball's inventor, Dr.

By 1940, teamwork had taken them to an international pinnacle. With no one left to lick, they disbanded.

James Naismith, saw them perform he said only: "The Grads have the greatest team that ever stepped out on a basketball floor."

When the Grads set out to defend their laurels, much of Canada heard the results in wonder (or jammed newspaper switchboards with requests for scores). Through the 1920s and '30s the Grads were a magnificent tonic for Canadians who vicariously confronted Goliath through this collection of girl Davids, the names of whom became legendary. To this day, many a man still feels a nostalgic twinge at the thought of, say, Noel MacDonald, more wondrous when the west was winning than Jean Harlow and Mae West and Ginger Rogers combined. Noel was tall and cool and statuesque and remote and inaccessible and she could shoot under pressure! She was the Grads' all-time leading scorer with 1,874 points in 135 games. In the spring of 1940 a contest was conducted among fans attending Grad games to select an all-time all-star team. "Unfortunately," Page once recalled, "it resolved itself largely into a popularity contest, inasmuch as thousands of fans had never seen some of the old-timers in action." Nevertheless, Noel MacDonald's 3,613 votes were seven hundred more than the runner-up received. And rightly so. What a queen! (I never saw her.)

The names of the Grads were as familiar to sport-minded Canadians as Babe Ruth's or Charlie Conacher's. Noel MacDonald's predecessor as captain was the strong and tireless Gladys Fry. Another great name was Margaret MacBurney, who played more

games than any other Grad, 164. And there was little, black-haired, flashing-eyed Babe Belanger (what a marvellous name for a basketball player), and steady, unflustered Etta Dann, and dimple-cheeked Kate MacRae, not only a Grad but the wife of the greatest defenseman in hockey, Eddie Shore. There was steady, heady Mabel Munton, and Elsie Bennie and Helen Northup and Mildred McCormack and Kay MacRitchie and Connie Smith and the Johnson sisters, Dorothy and Daisy. In that first international series when the Grads beat the Cleveland Favorite-Knits Dorothy Johnson was a mere seventeen; she scored seventeen points in the second game, which the Grads won, nineteen to thirteen.

That was in 1923, when the Grads had already been established for eight years. In 1915, when Page formed the first team, he did so quite by accident. Indeed, except for a decision by Page's assistant, there would likely never have been an Edmonton Grads dynasty at all. Page had arrived in Edmonton in 1912, when he was twenty-five, to take charge of commercial courses in city high schools. He was a graduate of Queen's University at Kingston, and had taught for six years in New Brunswick and St. Thomas, Ontario, where he coached the relatively new game, basketball. (It was less than twenty years old; Dr. Naismith, another Canadian, had introduced it at the YMCA in Springfield, Massachusetts, in 1891.)

In 1914 Page was placed in charge of commercial classes at a new school, McDougall Commercial High, where he organized basketball teams as a physical-training activity. He offered his bachelor assistant, Ernest E. Hyde, the choice of instructing either the girls or the boys. Hyde, in a decision that was to have international repercussions, chose to drill the boys. Thus Page had charge of the girls. While construction of the school was being completed, games were played outdoors. Page's team won the city and the high-school and the provincial championships, and the following spring, though most of the girls were to graduate, they decided to stay together. Since they were graduates of the commercial course at McDougall, they formed the Commercial Graduates Basketball Club on June 15, 1915. Though they wore a large gold C in script on their atrocious black middies, they soon were known only as the Grads.

Page organized what amounted to a farm-club system for training new players. He had junior and senior teams in the school, and formed the Gradettes for graduates not yet sharp enough for the Grads. Naturally, such organization easily overwhelmed the makeshift local opposition. Except in 1921, when the university team beat the Grads, the provincial play-downs were walk-overs. Even in 1921 the Grads *almost* won. They took the championship game seventeen to thirteen, but the university coach protested that a Grad player, Connie Smith, was still a student at McDougall and therefore not eligible to play as a graduate. The game was replayed, with Connie a spectator, and the university team won, twenty-nine to twenty-three. In later years non-graduates did play for the Grads, but in the team's twenty-five-year history only two players, Gladys Fry and Mae Brown, were never students at McDougall Commercial High School.

During their first seven years the Grads attracted little attention, largely because their games were local except for an occasional provincial challenge from Camrose or Wetaskiwin or Calgary. But in 1922 they were invited to engage the London Shamrocks in the first east-west final. The London sponsors could guarantee only six hundred dollars towards expenses for the trip, which by Page's estimate would cost at least a thousand. So each girl contributed twenty-five dollars, a few local merchants made up the rest, and the players carried lunches and sat in the daycoach to avoid the cost of the dining-car and sleepers. Only six girls made the trip – the Johnson sisters, both of whom were stenographers; Winnie Martin, a school teacher and team captain; Eleanor Mountfield, a bookkeeper; and Connie Smith and Nellie Perry, both stenographers.

When the Grads overwhelmed the London girls and won subsequent exhibition games in Toronto and St. Thomas, the legend of the Grads began. Cheering crowds replaced the indifferent legions at home in Edmonton. Thousands crowded into the CN station to greet them and lined Jasper Avenue along a parade route to the Macdonald Hotel, where the mayor gave medals to the conquering heroines. A local promoter underwrote a guarantee of eighteen hundred dollars to bring the Cleveland Favorite-Knits to Edmonton for the first international series as the Grads embarked upon their enduring climb from peak to peak. In 1933 a North American championship series was inaugurated between the national champions of the United States and Canada, to be played annually in Wichita, Kansas. The Grads, of course, were Canada's perennial representatives. It was here, at long last, that defeat finally overtook them.

The American champion in the inaugural year was a team from Oklahoma called the Durant Cardinals, who whipped the Grads in three straight games. This was the longest losing streak in their history. The Grads desperately wanted a rematch, of course, but for three years the Durant Cardinals kept losing the American final to the Tulsa Stenographers, a big tough team that included five All-Americans. The Grads gained only token solace by whipping the Stenos, who were an average of fifteen pounds heavier and two inches taller. The Grads beat them three straight games in 1932, and three out of four in 1935 and again in 1936.

But in 1936 sponsorship of the Durant Cardinals was taken over by an Arkansas oil company, and they were renamed the El Dorado Lion Oilers. As such, they challenged for the Underwood Trophy and this finally gave the Grads the chance they had been seeking for three years.

New frontiers of excitement were explored in Edmonton when the series opened on May 28. More than seven thousand people wedged into the arena and thousands more listened to the play-by-play account on radio station CJCA. Unbelievably, the peerless Grads were beaten, forty-four to forty. Incredibly, with one minute to play in the white-hot tension of the second game, the Arkansans held a two-point lead.

Then Noel MacDonald took a quick bounce-pass from little Babe Belanger and dropped in a lay-up shot to tie the score with twenty-seven seconds to play.

And then the final seconds were ticking away and the Grads had the ball and they moved it down the court as they had so many hundreds and thousands of times before . . . Margaret MacBurney to Etta Dann to Babe Belanger to Noel MacDonald to Belanger to MacDonald who on the last tick of time lofted a thirty-five-foot shot that hit the rim, bounced high in the air, settled back on the rim, rolled around it – and dropped in. That broke the challenge. The Grads ran off with the third and fourth games easily. No team ever really bothered the Grads again.

In 1940, after twenty-five years, J. Percy Page disbanded his magnificent creation. There was a war, the Royal Canadian Air Force had moved into the Edmonton Arena, and there was no place to play.

There was nobody left to lick, either.

TRENT FRAYNE

STRATEGY

Horse races often turn on a jockey's instant judgements. (*At left:* Canada's brilliant young Ron Turcotte.) And in other sports, too, victory is sometimes not to the fastest or strongest—but the wiliest.

In guiding a football team or a thoroughbred horse, brains count more than brawn

In 1956, when he was 29, Bud Grant (*left*, with earphones) was elevated from his job as a pass-catching end and defensive stalwart of the Winnipeg Blue Bombers and made coach. It was good strategy on the part of the Bombers' management. Grant, a quiet, thoughtful man, immediately proved himself one of the best strategists in football. In 1958, Grant's team started a streak of four Grey Cups in five years—a record.

In 1941, when he was 23, Frank Merrill was stricken with tuberculosis. He spent the next two years in a sanitarium. On his release Merrill turned to training race-horses, and by the middle 1950s, horses he trained and whose strategies he plotted were winning more races than those of any other trainer in North America. One of Merrill's specialties is to claim horses that have broken down under other trainers and nurse them back to health and the winner's circle.

In 1965, when he was 58, Johnny Longden (*below*, aboard a winner in England) became the first jockey in history to have ridden 6,000 winning horses. Longden had won his first race in 1927, and gone on to ride Whirlaway, Noor, Swaps, and his own favorite, Count Fleet. By number 6,000 he no longer had the strength or reflexes of the younger jockeys, but his knowledge of how to ride a race — his sense of strategy — was unsurpassed.

The man who discovered Frank Mahovlich (among others)

All strategy isn't worked out during the play, or even immediately before it. Bob Davidson, the firm-jawed man in the foreground at right, was a valuable and diligent player for the Toronto Maple Leafs before he became a valuable and diligent scout for new Leaf talent. In 1953, for example, Davidson saw Frank Mahovlich playing minor hockey. Mahovlich was 14. The Leafs' instructions: get him at any cost. Davidson did, by offering Mahovlich, among other things, a free education. Davidson still won't reveal every plot he used to sign the young Mahovlich. But another team that was trying to get him vainly offered to buy his father a fruit farm. Mahovlich was only one of the Davidson discoveries who helped Toronto win three successive Stanley Cups in the 1960s.

The smartest player in hockey's history? Most experts would agree on Frank Nighbor, centre for Pembroke, Vancouver and Ottawa, winner of the first Hart trophy (1924), the first Lady Byng (1926) and inventor of the pokecheck.

The cleverest hockey coach? It would be hard to match the record of Dick Irvin, who won the Stanley Cup with two different teams — Toronto Maple Leafs in 1932, Montreal Canadiens in 1944, 1946 and 1953. Irvin coached in the NHL from 1930 to 1955, just before his death. He was one of the game's most liked and respected figures.

The most knowledgeable Canadian ball-player? George (Mooney) Gibson, iron-man catcher for the Pittsburgh Pirates who, after his retirement as a player, managed the Pirates from 1920 to 1922, and again from 1932 to 1934.

The master strategist of early Canadian sport, and one of Canada's greatest athletes: Toronto's world-famous sculler Ned Hanlan.

NED HANLAN

The first world champion of anything!

Cold rain drizzled through a veil of mist on the morning of November 15, 1880, in London, England. But no weather could keep the sporting fans at home. By what a Canadian correspondent described only as "a very early hour," the banks and bridges of the Thames along the historic four and a quarter miles of the Henley course were "peopled with a noisy, hustling crowd." The event the crowd was waiting for was a match race between the Canadian sculling champion, Ned Hanlan, and the Australian, Edward Trickett. To the winner would go the title of champion of the world. Already, the meeting between Hanlan and Trickett had been called "the race of the century."

The fortunes of rowing have fallen so low since the

beginning of the twentieth century that it is difficult for the sports fan of the 1960s to realize the prestige rowing once had. In England, Europe, the United States and Canada between the 1870s and the turn of the century, rowing drew crowds larger than those that attend Grey Cup games in Canada now. Purses for single-scull races reached four, five, six thousand dollars, and betting was as free and fast as it has since become on horse-racing. In the decades before the Olympic Games were revived (in 1896), when boxers, say, seldom travelled beyond the next county or state, rowing was *the* international sport. The world championship of rowing was the first real world championship of anything, and the race that young Ned Hanlan

The artist called this "The great Hanlan-Plaisted boat race, Toronto." It was 1874. Hanlan, as usual, won.

of Toronto was about to contest on that bleak November morning was the most important sports event in the world.

Hanlan was not the first Canadian oarsman to compete at the international level. In no country was rowing more popular or more advanced than in Canada. From the year of Confederation until the turn of the century it was the nation's major sport. In 1867 a four-oar crew from Saint John, New Brunswick, rowing a heavy, home-made shell, won first prize of three thousand francs at the Paris Exposition, defeating crews from England, France, Germany and the U.S. (Three years later a British crew from the Tyne travelled to Lachine, Quebec, and there finally defeated Saint John's world-champion "Paris Crew" before a crowd of fifty thousand. Feelings in Canada ran so high that the Montreal *Star*'s account of the English crew's victory began, "No one comes from Saint John today; we are all Englishmen," and papers everywhere were full of explanations and apologies for weeks afterward.)

But it was Hanlan who brought Canadian rowing to its peak. Even before his match race with Trickett for the world's title, Hanlan was recognized as the greatest single-sculler Canada had yet produced. And even if he had retired before that race – he was twenty-five in 1880 – his record would still tower over those of rowers who have emerged since. Hanlan was the second son of a storekeeper on the islands that enclose Toronto harbour. As a boy he rowed himself back and forth three-quarters of a mile to a mainland school every day. At eighteen he raced in a shell for the first time and won the amateur championship of Toronto Bay. At nineteen he added the championship of nearby Burlington – now Hamilton – Bay. At twenty he turned professional, accepting a challenge to race a mile for a hundred dollars. At twenty-one he rowed at Philadelphia in a race held to celebrate the centennial of the Declaration of Independence, and he beat the best oarsmen in America and two of the best from England. At twenty-two he became the champion sculler of Canada. At twenty-three he won the formal American title. And at twenty-four, the year before his race with Trickett, he became the British champion.

The most striking thing about Hanlan was his size. For an oarsman he was almost ridiculously small: five feet, eight and three-quarters inches tall (the Australian Trickett stood six-feet-six) and weighing only a hundred and fifty pounds. But the muscles of his slim, compact body were so well conditioned that, as one English fan recorded, "the more clothes he took off the bigger he got." Hanlan made up for his lack of size by developing both style and brains. His rowing stroke was as distinctive as, in later eras of sports, Babe Ruth's swagger or Arnold Palmer's swing. In the eyes of some critics everything about his style was wrong but the results. As one expert wrote: "He humps like the patient camel, slivers out, doesn't go through, hunches and spats the water. But the boat travels." Hanlan's unusual hump-backed crouch was perfect for the sliding seat, which came into use in the early 1870s when he was emerging as a champion. He pulled evenly, so that, as still another rowing writer observed, "his boat seemed to be pulled through the water on a string" instead of lurching along. The sliding seat had the effect of lengthening his arms and stroke, and giving him a longer sweep.

The second weapon in Hanlan's arsenal, though, was even more important. It was strategy, and in single-sculls races, usually held over courses of four or five miles, strategy was as vital as style or strength. Just as no one can run a middle-distance race full out all the way, no one could row five miles at his top speed. Deciding when to make a move mattered almost (though of course not quite) as much as the ability to carry it out. And Hanlan was a master strategist. His sense of pacing was acute: although he is still considered by some experts to have been the fastest single-sculler in history, he often rowed only – and precisely – fast enough to win. But his sense of psychology was even sharper. He was so adroit at embarrassing, annoying and even humiliating his opponents that he might have been known not only as Canada's first world champion but also as Canada's, and perhaps the world's, first true Gamesman.

In his race against Trickett, Hanlan used Gamesmanship to perfection.

Just before noon the fog on the Thames lifted, exposing smooth, clear water on the course. Trickett appeared first. According to the press accounts of the day, he looked a trifle off his usual weight. An anonymous correspondent of the *Canadian Illustrated News* thought his appearance was "care-worn." It might well have been. For weeks the newspapers, egged on by the cocky Hanlan and his confident Canadian backers – who were, of course, employing the first rules of Gamesmanship – had been full of stories of Hanlan's earlier accomplishments and fine conditioning, and Hanlan was a heavy favourite in the betting. One story even had it that Hanlan, a notoriously fast starter, was

a three-hundred-to-one favourite to be first under Hammersmith Bridge, roughly a third of the way down the course. For the race, the Australian stripped to his bare torso; Hanlan, who appeared on the river a few minutes later, was wearing his familiar blue shirt – the shirt that had earned him the newspaper nickname of the "Boy in Blue."

At half past twelve the contestants took their positions and the starter gave the shout of "go." Instantly Hanlan took the lead. Before they had covered the first quarter-mile the Canadian boat was half a length in front, and Trickett moved over near one shore. Hanlan was pulling a smooth thirty-three strokes to the minute, while Trickett was pulling thirty-six. Trickett began casting worried glances over his shoulder to check the length of Hanlan's lead. By Hammersmith Bridge it was a clear three lengths, gladdening the hearts of the three-hundred-to-one players (if there were any). As the bow of his shell sped under the bridge "like an arrow on the wing," one reporter wrote, "that structure groaned beneath a dense mass of excited people, who cheered as if each was gifted with lungs of brass."

Here, Hanlan threw in a powerful Gamesman's ploy. Suddenly, with his lead at three lengths, he stopped rowing. At the bottom of Chiswick Eyot, the *Canadian Illustrated News* reported, he "lay back in his shell with the most perfect nonchalance, lazily paddling first with one scull and then with the other," while the straining Trickett sped to catch him. When the Australian boat was within one length, Hanlan, refreshed, calmly picked up the stroke again, and opened a new lead of three lengths.

Again and again he indicated his scorn of his opponent. Just past Chiswick Church, fifteen minutes after the start of the race, Hanlan eased up to chat with William Elliott, the man he had beaten for the British title the previous year, who was observing the world's championship race from a shell of his own. By now, Trickett's fury must have been blinding. But Hanlan, the relentless Gamesman, refused to stop playing with him. As he passed the Bull's Head, the hotel where he and his Canadian contingent were staying, he stopped rowing to wave a handkerchief at the crowd. Then, before he regained his full speed, he appeared to collapse in his seat, slumping forward, letting his oars drift. But as Trickett pulled within a length of him Hanlan sprang upright, waved to the crowd and sped on his way. "A roar of laughter greeted this feat," one newspaper reported, "and it was some minutes before the intense excitement created by it abated."

Hanlan completed his humiliation of Trickett in the last lengths of the race. With Trickett pulling futilely in his wake, he rowed several strokes with one oar, then several with the other, zig-zagging easily across mid-stream until he coasted home to the first world championship a Canadian ever won.

Hanlan's victory, of course, was first of all a feat of athletic excellence. The *Sporting Life of London* said: "His sculling was worth travelling a hundred miles to see." But his daring, swashbuckling Gamesmanship – so many years before that word was invented – added to the dimensions of his triumph. Two years later Trickett challenged him again, and they met on the Thames in May of 1882 for a stake of five hundred pounds. This time, Hanlan's psychological demolition of the giant Australian was complete. After pulling away to win by nearly a minute and a half, Hanlan turned around the finishing buoy and rowed back to meet his opponent. When he was almost even with Trickett, Hanlan spun his shell around, and sculled off across the finish line ahead of his opponent for the second time in one race. Trickett never rowed in an important race again.

Hanlan's successes continued until 1884, when he was finally beaten by a two-hundred-pound Australian blacksmith named William Beach. Beach beat him twice that year on the Paramatta River in Australia. While some Canadian papers attempted to make excuses for Hanlan, the truth is that he was simply outrowed. He had met his match. At twenty-nine, he was unable to make up by strategy what he had to give away in youth and strength. The next year he lost his American championship. Later he regained it, but lost it again. In 1887 he lost a third time to Beach. Though he rowed competitively and in exhibitions until 1897 – he became a famous trick sculler – his champion's touch was gone. His record is still unsurpassed. In all he rowed some three hundred and fifty races, and he lost only about half a dozen. In nearly every one of his victories his sense of strategy played an important part.

No account of Ned Hanlan's career as strategist and oarsman would be complete without some mention of the most famous series of matches he took part in. In some eyes, this series marked the beginning of the end of single-sculling's respectability as a major sport. In 1952, Samuel Hopkins Adams, writing in *Holiday* magazine, called it "The Scandal That Killed A Sport." The question the matches posed was the most serious one any sport can raise: was Hanlan a victim of – or even a partner in – the ultimate and ultimately distasteful Gamesman's ploy, the attempt to rig a race?

The series was between Hanlan and an American sculler named Charles Courtney. Courtney had been as prominent an amateur oarsman as Hanlan had been a professional. In 1876 he had won the amateur title at Philadelphia while Hanlan was winning the professional title. But they had never rowed against each other. By the time Courtney turned professional the public was clamouring for a match. Their backers jockeyed for more than a year before coming to terms. Then, in 1878, they agreed to a match at Lachine, and Hanlan won – but only, Courtney's fans felt, because Courtney had encroached on Hanlan's lane. A re-match was scheduled for Mayville, New York, in October of 1879, a little more than a year before Hanlan was to meet Trickett in London.

Mayville was a small resort town on Chautauqua Lake. The proposed match between Courtney and Hanlan transformed it. Steamboat lines planned special excursions along the course. Special trains brought sportsmen by the thousand into town along a special spur line. A grandstand with seats for fifty thousand was erected. The race was to be for a purse of six thousand dollars, and the betting among the fans was feverish. At first the odds favoured Hanlan, but on the day before the race, according to Samuel Hopkins Adams, betting sentiment swung to Courtney: 100-90, 100-80, 100-75, and, finally, "there was word of two-to-one money to be had from frightened Canadians in their efforts to hedge."

The race never took place. On the night before, while the streets of Mayville were alive with holidaying fans, someone broke into Courtney's shed and sawed in half both his racing shell and his practice boat. The next morning was turmoil. Courtney refused to use an unfamiliar boat. Accusations flew. Courtney's backers accused Hanlan of having been living too highly and of being afraid of Courtney's faster practice times. Hanlan's backers accused Courtney of sawing his own boat. Both sides were accused by rumour of having tried to make agreements for a rigged outcome. All bets were cancelled, the purse was withdrawn, and the crowds went home frustrated and embittered.

The full story of what happened to Courtney's boats has never come out, although the literature of sculling is full of speculation. There has never been any evidence that Hanlan indulged in wrongdoing – even though, for instance, a Toronto *Globe* writer had worried about his chances of winning after "hippodroming around the country with a couple of pugilists and . . . training out with the rougher classes of sports." Hanlan's carefree approach to training, it seems in retrospect, was just one more facet of his cocky Gamesmanship. It is hard to see him being afraid of Courtney's times. When Courtney refused to appear, Hanlan rowed the course anyway, and with no opponent to use his ploys on he clocked the fastest time ever recorded for five miles. Later, Courtney did appear for a rematch at Washington, D.C. And – although Courtney pleaded poor health – Hanlan left him far behind.

Certainly the people of Toronto never questioned Ned Hanlan's skill or honesty. Until his death at fifty-two he was a famous and popular figure in the city. For two terms he served as an alderman. A point on the islands where he learned to row still bears his name. And a twenty-foot statue on the grounds of the Canadian National Exhibition – surely the only statue of a sculler in the world – still honours Canada's first Gamesman.

PETER GZOWSKI

SPEED

Of all the ingredients mixed into sports, none matches
SPEED in bringing the roaring rise from the crowd — and the hushed awareness
of near disaster. This driver (at Mosport, Ont.) lived.

Three fast men and a very fast girl

Fritz Hanson, a little powerhouse from Minnesota whose toes twinkled as he bobbed and danced and sidestepped with a football tacked against his sleeve, became as renowned in the west as Marquis wheat when he helped Winnipeg to the West's first Grey Cup. In Hamilton on an icy field in 1935, Hanson blinded 'em with footwork.

The sports world was astonished and set the feat down as a fluke when Percy Williams *(below)* became the world's fastest human in the 100 metres sprint at the 1928 Olympics. Then the shy Williams added the 200 metres gold medal and there really wasn't much left to sputter about, not even his melodramatic finishing style.

Charlie Gorman, with the long smooth gliding locomotion of effortless power, was the least publicized world champion of the 1920s. He won four world titles and tied for a fifth, broke two world records and equalled a third in five world meets in 1927 alone. Inspired sportswriters — those who'd heard of him — called Gorman the Man with the Million Dollar Legs and/or the Human Dynamo.

Other countries downgrade our abilities as persistently as we do ourselves, it seems. Thus, when Anne Heggtveit of Ottawa won an Olympic gold medal whooshing down a mountain at Squaw Valley in 1960, the only people more surprised than the favoured Austrians were, naturally, Canadians.

Ron Stewart was an anachronism, a five-foot-six ball-carrier in a Brobdingnagian world of modern 250-pound tacklers. But in the 1962 Grey Cup game at Vancouver, Stewart's speed and daring confounded the Goliaths of the Edmonton defense. Ottawa Rough Riders won the national championship, and Stewart won a sports car as the game's outstanding player.

The day
Bill Crothers made
Bruce Kidd run

Track became glamorous in the late 1950s with the emergence of Bruce Kidd and, a little later, Bill Crothers as runners of world calibre. Largely because of them, youngsters who'd been drawn to hockey and football turned to track for their kicks. Kidd, whose best distance was three miles, tried to break the four-minute-mile barrier in 1960, with Crothers pacing him. He missed by 2.2 seconds but afterward hugged Crothers (right) for his effort. By the 1964 Olympics injuries had slowed Kidd, and Crothers emerged as our top runner. He was second to world-record-holder Peter Snell in the 880 at Tokyo, and later his conqueror.

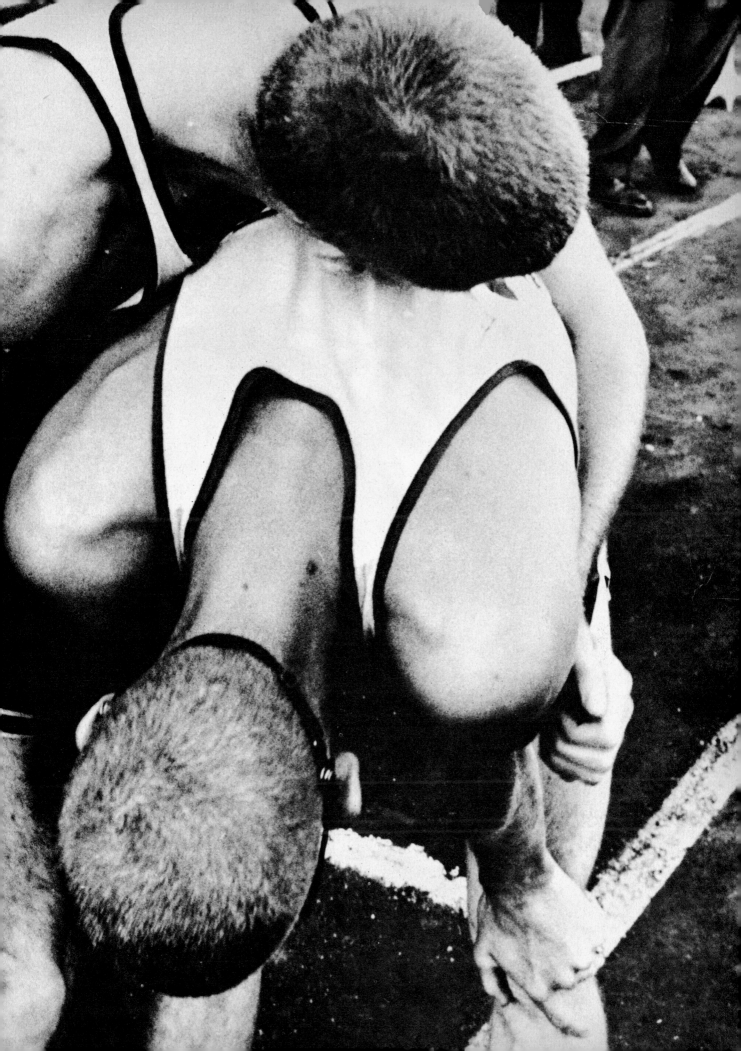

The fastest sleepy man in sport

What's the matter with the Big M?
That's what they wanted to know
in hockey's tower of babble,
Maple Leaf Gardens, through many
a Saturday night in the early
1960s. There were no halfway
measures with Frank Mahovlich, who
either soared to heights of
blurring speed and grace or
seemed to be asleep. When he was
flying, as he was in 1961,
he scored 48 goals in 70 games.
When he was taxiing, as he was in
1960, he scored 18 goals. He
always kept the natives restless.

NORTHERN DANCER

Running a hole in the wind

It was just past two o'clock in the hushed morning hours of May 6, 1964, and, as usual, the stocky Canadian-bred colt named Northern Dancer was champing for his breakfast, throwing his head impatiently and occasionally thumping the side of his stall with a hoof. The air outside the low grey barn at Churchill Downs was soft and warm, and far to the west a sheet of pale lightning glowed for an instant in the Kentucky sky.

Gnarled and bent, Willie Brevard shuffled towards the Dancer's stall with a pail of fresh water in one hand and a bucket of oats fortified with vitamins in the other. Brevard had been Northern Dancer's groom for most of the six months since his owner, E. P. Taylor, had shipped the colt from Toronto to New York, and thence to Florida for the winter racing season.

Now the groom, his dark face scowling under a battered serge cap, unlatched the stall's wire door, set down the pails and – gingerly – took the horse's bridle. He avoided a nip as the colt tossed his head a few times, and led him around for his breakfast. The Dancer's muscles glistened in the half-light cast by widely separated bulbs along shedrow. A pastel yellow blanket clung to the colt's nearly chestnut pelt – a solidly built and blocky colt with a mane and square-cropped tail of black, three white stockings, and a diagonal white blaze slashing down his nose from forelock to left nostril. He stretched a thick neck to his food, ate and drank contentedly for ten minutes, then sprawled down in the straw and went to sleep.

At six o'clock, with dawn breaking on a slate grey morning, Brevard roused the Dancer again, led him on a slow loosening walk around the barn, then returned him to his stall. At ten o'clock the colt ate more oats, and at four in the afternoon his trainer, Horatio Luro, a tall, suave Argentinian with an auburn pencil-moustache and thin reddish hair, went to the stall and rubbed him down with an alcohol-and-water solution. Luro felt this would refresh the colt, just as he believed that feeding him every eight hours allowed him to digest his food properly before a race on big days like this one, or before his early-morning works on off days. So although it was not a common practice among horsemen, Luro had instructed the groom to feed the horse each day at two in the morning, at ten, and at six in the evening.

Now Northern Dancer was ready. Brevard took his shank and led him on the long walk to the paddock beneath the swarming grandstand, half an hour before the running of the ninetieth Kentucky Derby, the most cherished and elusive and sentiment-inflicted horse race on the North American continent. Around the paddock, where a dozen three-year-old thoroughbreds were being saddled, a boisterous detachment of the hundred thousand or more spectators who were in the stands that day craned and jostled to see the horses.

Churchill Downs, Derby day, 1964: at the first turn the Dancer was sixth, still a mile from glory.

The air around the cramped square of tanbark was the same mint-scented mixture of bedlam, booze and nostalgia that always culminates with the running of the historic race late in the afternoon of the first Saturday of every May.

On this overcast day, the two favourites in the field of twelve were Hill Rise, the champion of California's winter season, and the little horse from Canada, the Florida champion who had swept the Flamingo Stakes at Hialeah, the Florida Derby at Gulfstream, and then the Blue Grass Stakes, a Derby tuneup at nearby Keeneland. Hill Rise was the crowd's first choice in the betting. This was partly for the left-handed reason that a Canadian-bred horse was said to be unlikely to last a mile and a quarter against horses of this calibre. But Hill Rise had also brought to the Derby a record of eight straight victories, including the Derby Trial the previous Monday. And then, too, the celebrated jockey Willie Shoemaker had decided to ride Hill Rise

in preference to Northern Dancer, although he had been the Dancer's rider in both the Canadian colt's victories in Florida stake-races. "I just think Hill Rise is a better horse," Shoemaker said. His place on the Dancer had been assigned to a controversial jockey named Bill Hartack.

As the crowd milled around the paddock, Luro bent to instruct Hartack, a sallow, sardonic little man wearing the silks of Mr. and Mrs. E. P. Taylor's Windfields Farm, a bright blue silk blouse with golden dots on the sleeves, and a gold silk cap over his crash helmet. "Keep him off the pace for about three-quarters of it," said Luro, his neck bulging as he made himself heard. "Move on the far turn, if you can, and be careful with the stick. His need is encouragement, never punishment. When he is hit, it can turn him sour."

Then, as the strains of *My Old Kentucky Home* waned in the leaden sky, the dozen thoroughbreds paraded up the track towards the starting gate at the top of the long home stretch. The betting windows closed; Hill Rise was six-to-five favourite, with Northern Dancer second choice at seven-to-two. The grey wooden grandstand, reaching the length of the stretch under its celebrated twin spires, was awash with faces. Across the track in the infield thousands more jammed towards the inside rail for the start of the punishing mile and a quarter test, which would take the horses once past the grandstand under the finish-line and then through a complete circuit of the one-mile rectangular track. It was a carnival crowd in the infield, with remnants of picnic lunches blowing across the green grass. People had started gathering there at eleven in the morning, when the first race in the long day had been run.

Beyond Kentucky, millions more watched the slow walk to the starting gate on television networks. In Canada, where Northern Dancer had become a kind of standard-bearer for the whole country, this Derby had become a television spectacle of more engrossing interest than the Grey Cup. Northern Dancer was a horse to cheer for. For one thing, he was small; you could see that as he stood there in the starting gate, wearing No. 7 and waiting for the break. He stood 15.2 hands, which means five-feet-one from the ground to the withers, or front shoulder blades. Hill Rise, No. 11, and another warmly regarded American horse, Quadrangle, were big, rangy blacks, each 16.2 hands – or four inches taller than the Dancer, as they stood in the gate.

But the Dancer was all drive and determination – a sort of equine bulldog, but pretty – and this could be seen even when the field broke far up the track and Hartack settled the Dancer easily into sixth place. You could see that the Dancer could, in the classic phrase, run a hole in the wind. Moving easily there, just off the fifth-place Hill Rise, he settled down to run. The Dancer's running style was to hang his head out in front of him, straining, and run with quick short sharp strides, not the classic flowing locomotion of the rangier kind but choppy and bobbing, and this style of his, this straining, all-out, grim and gallant style, struck a warm chord in anybody who watched him run. Northern Dancer refused to quit when he was running. That is what thoroughbred racing is all about, and that was the source of his amazing appeal.

Even standing still – and he wasn't now, of course, flowing easily along towards the clubhouse turn in sixth position – even standing still, he was something. A veteran journalist in Florida wrote after the Dancer won the Flamingo Stakes there, the first hundred-thousand-dollar race ever won by a Canadian horse: "This is a bold colt, an impudent, eye-catching rascal. He has character and a strangely disturbing personality. If you're an admirer of thoroughbred horses, you will fall in love with Northern Dancer at first glance. There's something about this colt that causes your heart to skip a beat. There's a dramatic intensity in his every restless movement. He exudes explosive excitement."

Now, though, he was in trouble. Northern Dancer was running close to the rail, Hill Rise outside him, and ahead of him was a wall of three horses behind the two front runners, Royal Shuck and Mr. Brick. The Dancer was trapped; Shoemaker, on Hill Rise, had him penned in with nowhere to go.

Here Hartack made the first of two significant decisions: he brought Northern Dancer off the rail in a sudden burst, taking Shoemaker and Hill Rise by surprise. Shoemaker had intended to keep the Dancer sealed, but now he couldn't get his bigger horse moving fast enough to prevent the smaller one's darting escape.

When this happened, the tens of thousands came alive with a great roar, and in a box on the first mezzanine Edward Plunket Taylor, the owner, jumped up, thrusting his right arm into the air, his round face ruddy as he cried out, his big heavy body straining.

Eighteen months earlier, this excited man might have lost Northern Dancer for twenty-five thousand dollars. In 1952 Taylor, as president of the Ontario Jockey Club, had bought and closed five old race tracks and consolidated thoroughbred racing in Ontario on three new or refurbished tracks, at a cost of thirty million dollars. He had also charged into the breeding industry, shopping for proven and distinguished bloodlines in the United States, England and Europe. But as he had expanded and flourished, he had realized, too, that he was causing undertones of annoyance among thoroughbred owners in Ontario, where he controlled the tracks and where the horses he bred soon were winning most of the big purses.

Taylor then instituted a plan of offering for sale the pick of his thoroughbred crop each year. First he settled on a price, based on breeding, for each of his yearlings. To keep fresh blood under his own racing colours he closed the sale when half the crop had been sold, and raced the horses that remained. Thus the first foal of the sire Nearctic and the broodmare Natalma (a daughter of the famous Native Dancer) was a colt priced at twenty-five thousand dollars in the 1962 sales. There were no takers, but this wasn't particularly surprising; despite his impressive breeding, the colt that became Northern Dancer was not a striking horse as a yearling.

"He looked pretty good as a weanling at Natalma's side," the racing manager of Taylor's Windfields Farm, Joe Thomas, once said, "but by the following autumn he was so short and so damned chunky that he was a real disappointment." Nor had there been anything prepossessing about him at birth, early in the morning darkness of May 27, 1961, when Natalma's first foal was registered at Taylor's National Stud Farm near Oshawa by Peter Poole, who cleaned off the colt, checked the clock at fifteen minutes past midnight, and noted in the stable diary: "A tight but normal foaling."

But nobody could mistake the Dancer's quality when he got to the races in his two-year-old year. Born in May and therefore a late foal – all thoroughbreds become one year older each January first, and breeders usually try to time the birth of foals to that date – he was kept from the races until August, 1963. He won five out of seven starts in Ontario and then went to New York's Aqueduct Park, where he won two more races, including the important Remson Stakes for two-year-olds.

Just before the Remson Stakes he had sustained a setback that might well have changed his life. This was a crack in the front left hoof, or quarter, and therefore called a quarter-crack. Until a few years ago there was no cure for such cracks, although some grew out, much as a split will in a human fingernail. During the 1950s a California blacksmith named Bill Bane searched for a substance that would patch but not hurt a living hoof, remaining locked in place while new growth came in. Ultimately he perfected a patch based on a rubber compound, and word of his success spread among blacksmiths. At Belmont Park, where Northern Dancer was stabled, Luro's blacksmith heard of Bane, and the stable mailed him pictures of the Dancer's crack. Bane flew to New York one morning in December and performed an eight-hour operation. Then he flew back to California with a thousand dollars in fee and expenses.

Bane had done his work well. The Dancer, who might have been on the shelf for six months or perhaps forever, missed no training and moved to Florida to undertake the three-year-old campaign which, on this afternoon in May, had led him to the top of the stretch, a quarter of a mile from the wire, in first place.

He had rounded the final turn, continuing his big move on the outside and passing the leading three. With a quarter of a mile to go, the race was so tightly contested that the first six horses thundered past the quarter-pole only three lengths apart. Here Hartack made his second significant decision. He remembered Luro's instructions (When he is hit, it can turn him sour) but, nevertheless, in his need Hartack decided to tap his mount lightly. Northern Dancer responded, bounding into the lead by two lengths. Shoemaker whipped Hill Rise, too, and the big black colt began his long run to overhaul the Dancer, now in a full drive over that grinding final three-sixteenths of a mile. The two horses were now in a test of the rawest element of sport, speed.

Hartack, delighted with Northern Dancer's response to the whip, hit him harder, on the left side to prevent him from lugging too close to the rail. With Hill Rise also answering the challenge, the real race was on, the real examination of courage, lungs and muscle. There comes a point when a contest of speed is reduced to complete simplicity; nothing counts but

moving the legs. Hartack hit the Dancer ten times left-handed in the final three-sixteenths of a mile, as Hill Rise slowly closed on the outside. Shoemaker received a tremendous effort from Hill Rise; little by little the gap narrowed as the two raced through the frantic Derby crowd, screaming from both sides of the long stretch. Hill Rise reached for the Dancer's flank, his girth, his shoulder, his neck.

Then the Dancer called on whatever elements combine to produce great thoroughbreds and brought forth more than he had already given. He didn't seem to run faster – he couldn't. He simply refused to yield any more track.

On the roof of the weathered grandstand a Canadian witness was aware that Hill Rise had run out of ground. Northern Dancer, his neck outthrust for the wire, his head bobbing, could not be caught. The witness found himself crashing his hands repeatedly onto a restraining railing, and shouting over and over, "He's going to make it! He's going to make it! He's going to make it!"

And, of course, he did.

Two weeks later, he did it again in the rich Preakness Stakes at Baltimore, the second leg of the "Triple Crown" of American racing. But in June he failed in his bid to become the first horse since Citation in 1948 to win all three legs of the crown; he was third to Quadrangle and Roman Brother. Then he came home in mid-June to win the Canadian classic, the 105th consecutive running of the Queen's Plate. A few weeks later, training at Belmont for the autumn season in the U.S., he rapped himself on the sheath that protects the tendon on the inside of the left foreleg, puncturing it slightly and precipitating a slight bow in the tendon itself.

"It's only a small bow," E. P. Taylor said hopefully after weeks of treatment. "A very small bow." But horsemen less involved emotionally repeated the ancient philosophy of the backstretch: a very small bow is like a slight case of pregnancy. Bowed tendons in great thoroughbreds are not a matter of degree; a bow strips a fraction of speed from a champion, the fraction that sets him apart.

In due course, then, Taylor decided to retire Northern Dancer to stud at Taylor's National Stud Farm, where the colt had himself been bred and foaled. His stud fee was set at ten thousand dollars for each service, and his book was quickly filled with the names of thirty-five broodmares, more than half of them owned by Americans.

The Dancer had proven what few horsemen had been able to believe. In his brief racing career, highlighted by the Derby victory in two minutes flat, a faster time than Gallant Fox or Cavalcade or Whirlaway or Carry Back or Citation or any of the other eighty-four Derby winners had achieved, he had proven that when faster horses are bred, there is no reason why they should not be bred in Canada.

TRENT FRAYNE

The Dancer's running style: big muscles, choppy stride.

INSPIRATION

Ken Doraty, a journeyman hockey player for Toronto, won instant immortality on April 3, 1933, by scoring in the sixth overtime period of Stanley Cup action, beating Boston Bruins 1-0. Many similar moments mark the history of sport: moments when a man, for reasons no one really understands, rises above the limits of his own skill.

At the age of 43, with the peak of his career well behind him. Vancouver's Stan Leonard shot the one tournament score that put him in the ranks of golf's finest professionals: 69-69-69-68 to win the 1958 Tournament of Champions at Las Vegas. Afterward, he revelled in some of the ten thousand silver dollars of prize money.

The best fight Yvon Durelle ever fought he lost — to Archie Moore, in Montreal, in December, 1958. But before he went down Durelle had the great Moore on the canvas four times. For one evening, Durelle glimpsed the greatness he never quite achieved.

Two lanky university students, George Hungerford and Roger Jackson, stunned the rowing world at the 1964 Olympics by winning the pairs without coxswain. It was Canada's first gold medal at the summer games since 1956 and, most remarkable of all, Hungerford and Jackson won it after rowing together only two weeks.

Four moments when everything went right

A horse named Willie the Kid won the 1940 King's Plate, for a purse of $6,720. It was the richest Canadian race of the year, and the richest race Willie the Kid ever won. It was, as a matter of fact, the *only* race Willie the Kid won in his life.

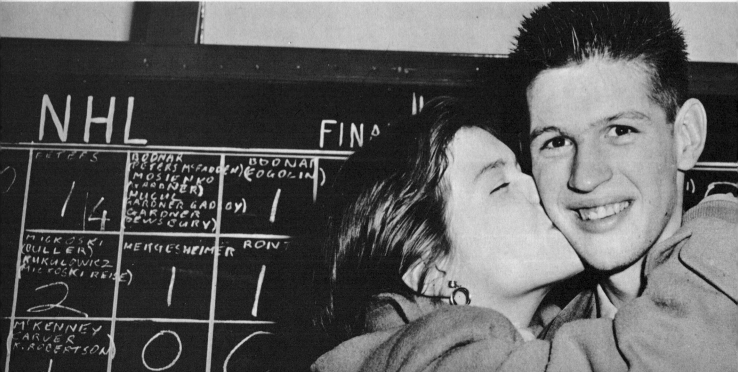

The faces of fleeting fame: three athletes on the best days they ever had

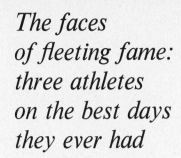

Joe Zuger was just another quarterback — good enough to make the Hamilton Tiger-Cat team in the early 1960s, never good enough to hold down the first-string job for more than a game or two at a time. It is impossible to say what happened to Zuger on October 15, 1962, but on that day he set one of the most astonishing records in Canadian football. Driving the Tiger-Cats to a 67-21 defeat of the Regina Roughriders, Zuger threw eight touchdown passes (four of them to a more consistent player than he, Garney Henley). For 60 minutes on that October afternoon, Joe Zuger was the most devastating passer in the professional game.

Eric Nesterenko was 19 on the night in the fall of 1952 when he played the second professional hockey game of his life. He was living the dream of every Canadian schoolboy: pulling on a Toronto Maple Leaf sweater and skating out to become part of Hockey Night in Canada. That night, he was almost the whole show: he scored two goals and just missed a third. His sister kissed him, and the hockey writers spoke of him as a coming superstar. But stardom never came; overconfident, he was cut by the Leafs, and despite a successful later career with the Chicago Black Hawks he never had another night in the NHL quite like his second one.

Ethel Catherwood, or as the folks back home called her, the Saskatoon Lily, was a fair high jumper — for a girl. She won a place on Canada's 1928 Olympic team easily enough, but at Amsterdam nobody expected her to do more than give it an honest try. She did all that and more: her final jump set a new world and Olympic record, at five feet, two and nine-sixteenths inches. What's more, that day she was a double threat. According to the New York *Times*, the Saskatoon Lily was "the prettiest of all the girl athletes" in Amsterdam that year.

RED STOREY

The fifteen-minute hero

In 1938, when he was twenty years old, Roy Alvin Storey was so big and rambunctious and rawboned that it took two nicknames to do him justice. Some people called him Red and some people called him Buster. Almost no one would have called him a football star. His older sister, Irene, had been the Storey family's outstanding athlete. Irene held the Canadian women's record for running 220 yards. In 1934, when Roy Alvin 'Buster' "Red" was sixteen years old and still fooling around with cornerlot football and baseball and junior hockey at home in Barrie, Ontario, Irene was the 60-yard champion of the British Empire Games. At seventeen Red left school and went to Leaside, a suburb of Toronto, to work in the railway yards. The next summer he met Ted Morris, the Toronto Argonauts' halfback (and later coach), who was a good little man himself but could recognize a good big man when he saw one, and Morris brought Storey out to Argonaut practice in the summer of 1936.

Storey's first seasons as a "club" player – what would now be called a semi-pro – were inauspicious. His rookie year was cut short by a shoulder separation. In 1937 he stayed with the Argos up to and through their Grey Cup victory, but, as he has since said, "I wasn't much help." Until the final quarter of the 1938 Grey Cup game, he was a substitute halfback.

Storey stayed with the Argos well after the 1938

season; he was a regular until 1942, and he was promising enough that two fully professional teams from the U.S. tried to lure him south. He was a talented baseball player, too, good enough to be invited to a big-league tryout. He also stood out at lacrosse; one night in Lachine, Quebec, he scored twelve goals in a single game. And he was a good if unspectacular hockey player for two American teams and, later, the Montreal Royals. But a football knee injury kept him from ever exploiting his full potential as an athlete, and in the early 1940s, when the knee could no longer stand up to the contact of the games he loved, he turned to refereeing hockey. He stayed in sports until 1959, when he quit in bitterness and frustration after his boss, the president of the National Hockey League, unwarrantedly questioned his courage during a wild Stanley Cup game. Throughout most of his career, Storey, the jack of all games, was a sort of peripheral figure in Canadian sports – there but not *really* there; a gifted and likeable man, familiar to almost everyone inside the sports world but scarcely noticed by the casual fan; the figurehead of nobody's personality cult, the endorser of nobody's shaving cream.

But he had his day: December 12, 1938, Grey Cup Saturday. For three-quarters of the game Storey sat in the accustomed obscurity of his sub's blanket while

WHEN ARGOS TAMED WINNIPEG

Every once in a while somebody streaks across the football record and leaves his mark with a standout performance that time will not erase. Saturday Red Storey did just that to pace Argos to a thrilling 30 to 7 victory over Winnipeg Blue Bombers in the Canadian final at Varsity Stadium. In the upper shot Storey (No. 64) can be seen easing up after crossing the Blue Bombers' goal-line with his third touchdown. In the lower picture the Barrie "redhead" is just gathering a lateral pass to start on one of his thrilling final chapter jaunts.

Sock Fund!

Sports Department's Drive to Help Out Star Santa Claus Fund Meeting With Great Response— Week-End Contributions

The sports department "Sock

CAGERS ROUGH IT UP IN BIG SIX TWIN-BILL

Simpson Grads and West End Purples Score Upset Wins

That the Big Six senior basketball league is down to serious busi-

Four of Tonight's Battlers Have Win Records to Protect

the better-known Argonaut players—men like Annis and Bill Stukus and Art West and Bob Isbister—fought a close, tense battle with the Winnipeg Blue Bombers. When Storey got off the bench, in the opening moments of the fourth quarter, Winnipeg was ahead by a score of seven to six. Storey tore the game apart. He played like a man inspired, and his inspiration lifted the whole Toronto team into one of the finest quarters of football ever played in Canada. Led by Storey, Toronto gained more yards in the final quarter than Winnipeg managed during the entire game. Counting an intercepted pass he ran back, Storey himself gained a hundred and ninety yards. He scored three of the Argonauts' four touchdowns, and he set up the other with his runback. The final score of the game that had been so close when he came in was thirty to seven.

What makes an athlete have a day like Storey's? At least a dozen things, from the accidents of luck to the psychology of being "up." No one really knows what brings all the factors together at once. A great athlete can go through his whole career without ever quite catching fire the way Storey did; yet a journeyman hockey player can suddenly score five goals in one game and then revert to near anonymity until he retires. But whatever causes it, when everything does go right for one man in one day it is one of the most exciting spectacles in sport.

Storey's display of heroics had an extra dimension. He was one member of an all-Canadian team—one of the last of such teams in a game that has grown increasingly American—and he was playing against a team stacked with imports. The skill that exploded in him that Saturday was a skill that had traditionally made Canadian football more distinctively exciting than the American version of the game: the ability of one man to carry a football past twelve other men, without a battalion of blockers. And even though the Grey Cup game has gone on in the years since to become the most ballyhooed show in Canadian sport, no chapter of its history makes more dramatic retelling than the game that Storey won all by himself.

It is worth looking at a little of the background. Part of the drama of Storey's game lay in its reflection of the rivalry between eastern and western Canada. This rivalry has been the heart of Grey Cup spirit almost from the outset. To a degree matched only—if at all—by a Stanley Cup final between Toronto Maple Leafs and Montreal Canadiens, the Grey Cup is a clash of regions. Each has its own characteristics, and at least one region, the west, has long resented the other. In the postwar years, some of the regional rivalry has been dulled. Rampant professionalism has taken some of the old-home-town appeal out of the game, and roaring prosperity, common to both eastern and western Canada, has taken out some of the resentment. The differences have become blurred. In 1938, though, the rivalry was at a zenith.

The first time a western team had presumed to challenge for the Dominion rugby championship was in 1911, the year the western league was formed. The east, quickly adopting the attitude of amused condescension that was to characterize so many of its future actions, dodged the challenge on a technicality involving the date of an annual meeting, and no team from west of Sarnia got a crack at the eastern champions until 1921. The first true all-Canadian final was between Edmonton Eskimos and Argonauts, played at Varsity Stadium in Toronto. The crowd was scarcely larger than the platoons of entertainers who perform at half-time during the hugely commercial Grey Cups of the 1960s; to easterners, the only championship that mattered was the local one. Argonauts lived up to everyone's expectations by winning easily. After absorbing a couple more solid lickings the westerners stopped bothering even to challenge. Then, in 1928, the citizens of Regina began to catch what Tony Allan, the Winnipegger who wrote Grey Cup Cavalcade, calls

"The Great Madness"—the fever that made football the national game of the west. That fall, Regina sent its Roughriders into the jaws of the Hamilton Tigers, and, though the Riders were soundly beaten, the "madness" began to spread through the west.

It was the west that Americanized Canadian football. As far back as 1921, two American college players travelled to Toronto with the Eskimos. By the middle of the 1930s, coaches and managers from the prairies were scouting the great football colleges of the American midwest. In 1935, when the Winnipeg Blue Bombers arrived at Hamilton to take on the Tigers, the Bombers had eight American stars in the line-up. And that team—the 1935 Bombers—changed the face of the Grey Cup for good. Led by their great halfback, Fritz Hanson, the Minnesota Reindeer, who ran back punts for the astonishing total of three hundred yards (all the while carrying a telegram from his mother in his shoe), the Bombers beat Hamilton eighteen to twelve, and the Grey Cup went west at last.

The east, though, had one more trick of legislation up its sleeve. With its long tradition of club and university teams, the east saw little need to import football players. The whole thing, in fact, struck easterners as just a little nouveau riche. The men Tony Allan calls the Old Guard of the Canadian Rugby Union moved to discourage imports by ruling that no one was eligible to play in future Grey Cup games unless he had lived in Canada for at least a year. Winnipeg, with its full quota from 1935, would still have qualified. But Regina, struck by a new wave of the "madness," had packed its own team with Americans for 1936, and beaten the Bombers for the western championship. The Roughriders refused to play without their imports, and the cup went back east by default.

The 1937 Grey Cup game, with Red Storey sitting on the bench, was a battle of kickers. Argonauts beat Winnipeg four to three, with the help of an intercepted pass in the last minutes. The defeat was a frustrating one for Winnipeg, and it proved little. Between seasons, Winnipeg fired its coach and began preparing for a new assault. The stage was set for a showdown.

On Grey Cup Saturday, 1938, Torontonians could have gone to Loew's Theatre to see Young Dr. Kildare with Lew Ayers in the title role and Lionel Barrymore as his father figure, Dr. Gillespie. Uptown, they could have seen the man who has since become the real Dr. Gillespie, Raymond Massey, playing a bearded Moslem warlord in Drums. FiFi D'Orsay was on stage at the Casino and Sonja Henie was skating at Maple Leaf Gardens. The Shadow was on the radio at seven-thirty that evening. Across the border, in Buffalo, the Peden brothers, Torchy and Doug, had just won a six-day bicycle race, and at home a young forward with the Toronto Goodyears, Punch Imlach, had just moved into the OHA scoring lead. The night before, Col. George Drew had been elected leader of the Ontario Conservative Party. A soaking rain fell on

Friday evening, but Saturday dawned mild and clear; the field was soft but not too slippery, and 18,846 people paid their way into Varsity Stadium at $1.50 tops. Children were allowed in for a quarter.

Of the crowd, perhaps three hundred were Winnipeggers who had travelled down especially for the game. The word downtown was that they had brought twenty-five thousand dollars in gambling money – "a lot of mazuma!" as the Toronto *Star* said. Odds that had been quoted at eight-to-five Argos in mid-week fell to six-to-five by game time.

For the first half, it looked as though a lot of the mazuma would be going back west. "I believe the feeling was that Argos had met their match," Lionel Conacher, the former great Argo star, remarked later. Early in the first quarter, Art Stevenson, the Nebraska medical student who was Winnipeg's quarterback, kicked from the Argos' thirty-five-yard line for a rouge. Shortly after, the Argos fumbled deep in their own end, but the Argo line, led by such stalwarts as George Hees, held. Winnipeg settled for a field goal by Greg Kabat, playing with freezing to dull the pain of a broken toe. Argos got the lead back briefly on a touchdown pass from Annis Stukus to Art West, but Stukus – who alternated with his brother Bill at quarterback and at kicking converts – missed the extra point. When Winnipeg marched deep down field late in the first half and got another field goal from Kabat, it was seven to five for the west.

In the first half, neither team had played strictly according to its form. The Argonauts, coached by Lew Hayman, were widely known as a razzle-dazzle team, and their favourite play was the extension end-run – two or three lateral passes, a specialty of the Canadian game, would shake the outside men loose down the sidelines. Winnipeg, now playing with six imports, favoured tactics more usually associated with the American game: more passing, crisper blocking around the line of scrimmage. But in the first thirty minutes, Winnipeg's hard-charging ends had kept the Argos up the centre, and Argos' tough linemen had held Winnipeg's two veteran running stars, Hanson and Eddie James, to short gains.

The third quarter was little different. Two Bill Stukus passes brought Argos to within twenty yards of the Winnipeg goal line, but Annis Stukus's field goal attempt was wide and low – good for only a single point. Winnipeg was still ahead by one point when the quarter ended, with Argos first-and-ten on the Winnipeg forty-three.

Storey, the bright number 64 on his double-blue uniform standing out clean from the huddle, took over the game almost as soon as he entered it. On the first play of the final quarter, the Argo halfback Bob Isbister passed to Annis Stukus for a fifteen-yard gain. On the next play, Storey broke to his right, taking a lateral on the run, with one man outside him as if for the patented extension play. But Storey sensed an opening inside, and quickly cut to his left. Five Winnipeg tacklers had a chance at him before he crossed the goal line, and the fifth knocked him off balance. But he staggered over, scoring the game's first running touchdown the first time he had the ball – twenty-eight yards from scrimmage. Annis Stukus converted, and Argos had the lead back, twelve to seven.

It was the end of the contest. On the next sequence, Storey picked off one of Stevenson's passes at the Winnipeg forty-five and darted through the broken field, without, of course, the benefit of blockers, to the four. Isbister lost six. But on the next play, Storey, running wide, lateralled to Ted Morris, and Morris was in to the one. The Argo line, already feeling the lift of Storey's inspired play, ripped a giant hole up the middle on the next play, and Storey went in easily for his second touchdown. Again Annis Stukus hit the convert.

Now trailing eighteen to seven, the Blue Bombers grew desperate. Stevenson began passing on every down, and hitting enough to move inside Argo territory. Within striking distance he sent the speedy Hanson deep into a corner and threw long and high to him. Isbister made a leaping interception and then, waiting until the last split second before Hanson hit him, lateralled perfectly to Storey. Storey headed for the sidelines. Legs churning, head back, the ball tucked firmly under his left arm, Storey ran a hundred-yard dash from the Argos' five to the Bombers' five, where he was knocked out of bounds by a desperation dive. On the first play, Bill Stukus flipped an easy pass to Bernie Thornton for the touchdown, and then kicked the convert.

Storey capped his day with one more touchdown. With three minutes left the Argos intercepted their third Stevenson pass of the quarter, then worked the ball to the Winnipeg nine, from where Storey ran straight up the centre to score. With Bill Stukus's convert, the score was thirty to seven. Fifteen of the points and all the lift had come from the substitute halfback.

Red Vail, an Argo lineman who was celebrating his thirtieth birthday and playing his last football game, was given the game ball, but everything else went to Storey. Fans carried him off the field and into the dressing room, where he received the personal congratulations of men like Sir Edward Beatty, the president of the CPR. That night Storey was the centre of attention at the Argonaut victory party at the Old Mill, in Toronto's west end, and on Monday, the sports pages were full of his accomplishment and his picture and his two nicknames. Before those Monday papers were out, though, Storey, who had stopped the Winnipeg bus after the game to trade sweaters with one of the losing players, and who had been able to think up nothing more memorable to tell the press than, "Gee, it's all so great I don't know what to say," had hitchhiked home to see his family in Barrie.

PETER GZOWSKI

Guts

Sometimes, because of a single honed skill, an athlete can climb above the caterwaul. But there's no way he can stay if he doesn't get up when getting up means he's apt to be knocked down again. That's what Lou Fontinato, the hockey player at left, did. And that's what he shared with many of Canada's great stars.

Greco slept, Meeker slugged, and Keys connected

Rocky Graziano, a study in ferocity, put across the unalterable *finis* in his fight with the pride of Montreal, the middleweight Johnny Greco, who found that guts alone are defenseless against a wicked right.

The scoreboard carries the final word in hockey, of course, but what it has to say often depends on who can intimidate whom. As Conn Smythe used to say, in essence: if you can't lick 'em in an alley you'll never beat 'em on the ice. Here's a one-time Smythe serf, Howie Meeker, illuminating his master's philosophy on an unidentified Canadien. The point is, if the Canadien didn't get to his feet and punch back, he was soon long gone.

By 1954, the west was weary of Grey Cup defeats, and Edmonton felt one more would be one too many. Outscored and weary after three quarters, they plugged away and tied the score when Jackie Parker turned a Montreal fumble into a field-length touchdown. Then Eagle Keys *(below)*, whose problem was a broken leg, hobbled on one limb to the field to snap the ball for the game-winning convert.

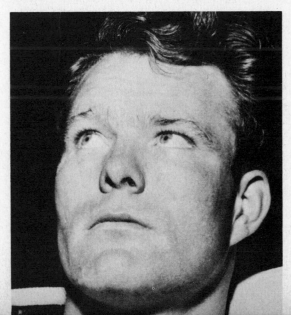

Howie Morenz had been the personification of the Forum battle-cry,
Les Canadiens Sont La! Late in a
waning career, he was traded to Chicago
and later to the Rangers. When he got
back to Montreal he briefly flashed
the form of the Stratford Streak of
old. Then a broken leg — and, some say,
a broken heart — led to his death.

Howie and Harry: two problems of pride

The widely whispered charge against
Harry Jerome, Vancouver's superior
sprinter, was that he'd shown all
the guts of a soft-shell clam in the
1960 Olympic Games. Trailing halfway
through the hundred metres, he
crumpled to the track, grasping his
thigh, his face contorted. What felled
him, a gossip of critics prattled,
was a severe case of impending defeat.
Jerome's contorted face turned
impassive in the months of finger-
pointing but on the track he gave it
everything he had. Within two years
he was co-holder of the world record for
the hundred metres, and nobody called
him anything but tough to beat.

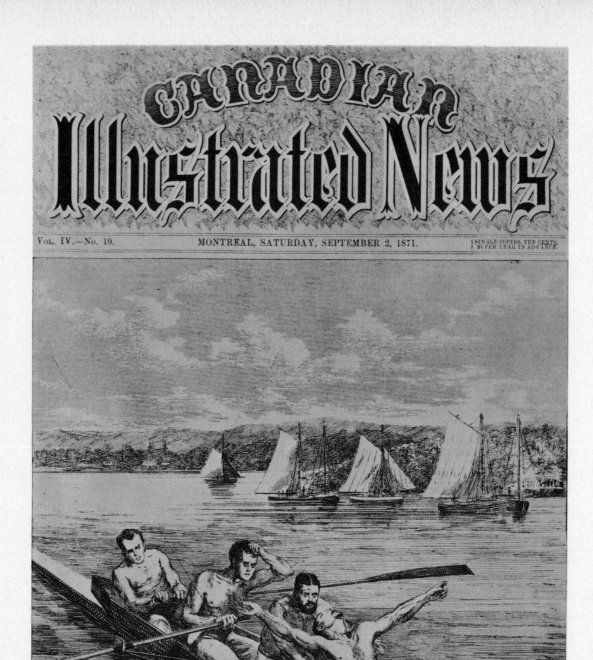

CANADIAN Illustrated News

VOL. IV.—No. 10.   MONTREAL, SATURDAY, SEPTEMBER 2, 1871.   SINGLE COPIES, TEN CENTS.
$4 PER YEAR IN ADVANCE.

It was 1871. The greatest sporting event of the year in the Maritimes was
the international boat race for the championship of the world. Canada's colours were
carried, as usual, by the famous "Paris" crew. But this time they lost the race
and their bow oarsman, Renforth, who pulled so hard trying to win that a few
yards past the finish line he fell back, dead of a heart attack.

JIMMY M^CLARNIN

The guts of a bugler

The two administrations of Jimmy McLarnin as welterweight champion of the world were notable for their brevity and for the fact that during them he never won a fight. Still, the rosy-cheeked little Irishman from Vancouver made an unforgettable imprint on the searing business that A. J. Liebling called, with a nice touch of irony, the Sweet Science.

There is surely no pursuit more fundamental than prizefighting. Its essential philosophy is as simple as it is brutal: stiffen the other guy or be stiffed. A certain amount of physical courage is required in all contact sports, but only boxing is predicated on an objective so basic as a punch in the nose. Like most fighters, McLarnin swapped scars with people so that he could

acquire a fistful of money and when he had enough – close to half a million dollars – he got out, one month before his twenty-ninth birthday in 1936, and lived happily ever after. He really did.

McLarnin flourished in and out of the ring in an era when it was extremely difficult to do either. He made his pile in the first five years of the 1930s, when most people were having trouble squeezing out an existence. Consequently, a lot of tough young guys were turning to the prize ring to make a buck, with the result that competition was probably fiercer then than at any time in boxing history.

Out of this guerrilla warfare, McLarnin emerged with sixty-three victories in seventy-three fights and with all his marbles. In 1950 he was elected to the ring's Hall of Fame, where he joined such illustrious men as John L. Sullivan, James J. Corbett, Jack Dempsey and Joe Louis. He took on and beat a swarm of gifted lightweights and welterweights when the United States was littered with them – Barney Ross, Young Corbett, Tony Canzoneri, Billy Petrolle, Kid Kaplan, Lou Ambers, Bud Taylor, Sammy Mandell, Fidel La Barba, Jackie Fields, Al Singer, and a sagging Benny Leonard unsuccessfully essaying a comeback. All these men won world championships except Petrolle, the old Fargo Express, and, ironically, it was in one of McLarnin's three fights with Petrolle that he took the most terrible beating of his life.

It is a singular fact that McLarnin met and defeated champions or former champions *fifteen* times but on thirteen of these outings his opponent was either an ex-champ, or if he was the champion, it was an overweight match in which the championship itself was not involved. Paradoxically, both times McLarnin won the welterweight title – from Young Corbett in Los Angeles in the spring of 1933 and from Barney Ross in New York in the autumn of 1934 – he lost his first defense, so that as champion he literally did not lick anybody.

McLarnin was easily the most colourful and by far the most prosperous of any Canadian fighter but it is conceivable that, pound for pound, he wasn't the best. That mantle might fall to one of four earlier Canadian boxers who became world champions, or even to a contemporary of his, the romantically christened Ovila Chapdelaine, who shucked that handle when he became a fighter and, as Jack Delaney, won the world's light-heavyweight championship in 1926. Delaney's name was forgettable, though; the light-heavyweight division has always been an anonymous one invented to hold tigers too big to be boxers and too small to be sluggers (Tommy Loughran was a magnificent exception). Delaney soon forsook the division to campaign with the heavyweights, among whom he was received with indifference.

McLarnin happened along a decade after boxing was made socially acceptable, in 1920, by a New York bill – the Walker Act – which legalized the manly art in that state and set off a chain reaction in most others. Even as late as World War I the game was in low repute; few women attended fights, which were usually held in smoky billiard rooms in men's clubs. It wasn't legal, but coppers and politicians could be persuaded to look the other way. After the war a few emancipated women began to appear at fights, although reformers still called boxing "brutal bear-baiting." Club members and their friends attended. Membership was usually fifteen dollars a year and a friend could become a temporary member for a dollar on the day of the fight. A couple of hundred dollars was a good purse for a fighter in the prewar era but prices were low, too. Eggs were twenty-three cents a dozen, tailored

suits were twenty-two dollars and newspapers were a cent apiece.

Three of Canada's five world champions flourished in this atmosphere. One was so wearied by it that he defended his championship in such exotic outposts as London, Dublin, Paris, Sydney and Melbourne. This was Noah Brusso, born in 1881 in the southern Ontario town of Hanover, who hid the nature of his occupation from his grey-haired mother by fighting under the name of a noted jockey, Tommy Burns. Burns, the fighter, was something of a wonder, five-foot-seven and 170 pounds. He became heavyweight champion in 1905 and relinquished the title in 1908 after nine successful defenses, usually against men big enough to be his father. Jack Johnson, who is often ranked as the best heavyweight of all time, caught up to Burns in Sydney and gave him such a thrashing that the brutality was stopped by police entering the ring in the fourteenth round.

At roughly the moment Johnson was destroying Tommy Burns, an Ontario bantamweight named Johnny Coulon became world's bantamweight (118 pounds) champion the easy way – the incumbent had outgrown the division. Coulon held the crown until 1914. Forty years later, when Nat Fleischer, boxing's most reliable historian, made his all-time ratings in each division, Coulon was listed number six.

In the same division, Fleischer ranked a Nova Scotian, George Dixon, as the greatest bantamweight of all time. Dixon forfeited the championship in 1892, when *he* outgrew the division. Then he won the featherweight championship (126 pounds) and held it for eight years more.

But, pound for pound, it's conceivable that the best of the Canadian fighters was one who never held a championship, Sam Langford of Weymouth, Nova Scotia. Langford, who had the silhouette of a gorilla and an actor's timing, brawled with and usually beat anybody he could catch, though at five-foot-six and 172 pounds he was sometimes compelled to give away ten inches and sixty pounds. Most boxers were as anxious to fight Sam as they were to find a case of Bubonic plague; this included Jack Johnson, who beat Langford once long before Johnson became champion, and stayed away from him thereafter. Perhaps, though, it wasn't distaste for punishment that made Johnson demur. "On a good night Sam is just liable to beat me or make it close," Johnson said in 1911, "and what's the sense of that for the kind of money we'd draw?" The majority of people resented the dominance of Negro fighters more publicly and patronizingly then than they did half a century later, when they weren't exactly applauding it, either.

To keep eating, Langford fought every three or four weeks for twenty-one years. He finally had to quit in 1923, when he was in his forties and blind in one eye. Fifteen times he fought Harry Wills, a man ten years younger, fifty pounds heavier and eight inches taller. Wills later hounded Jack Dempsey for a championship bout but earned only a series of rebuffs. Once, in New Orleans, Wills hammered Langford to the floor nine times in the first four rounds but could not keep him there, and in the nineteenth round was himself knocked out by the bloodied Langford.

Langford, who arrived on the scene twenty years too soon, missed the gold mine that legality and Dempsey created of the prize ring. On Dempsey's impact the whole beak-busting industry flourished, big men and small, and it was into this bristling milieu that McLarnin sprang in the mid-1920s, a baby-faced roughneck, the gamest and the toughest Canadian of the modern, or what might be called the legalized, era of assault and battery.

McLarnin wasn't a Canadian at all, in the strict sense, but he grew up here and set the pattern of his future here, so we claim him. He was born in Belfast just before the Christmas of 1907, the son of an Irish butcher who had ranched in Alberta, then returned to his homeland to marry. Jimmy was three when the family moved back to Canada, where ten of the dozen McLarnin children were born. They settled first on a farm west of Moose Jaw, and after six years moved to Vancouver. There, Jimmy's father opened a second-hand furniture store near the docks.

The brood got a strict Methodist upbringing from their mother. "I never had to be told that wine, women and song would ruin a boxer," Jimmy once said. "It had been drummed into me that wine, women and song could ruin *any*body." Still, he was no choir-boy. As the oldest child he sold papers on the waterfront, bloodied kids and got punched in return long before puberty. When he was eleven his father gave him two pairs of boxing gloves and he started down Union Street with the notion of taking on a kid at every corner. The first kid he beat. At the second corner he got his ears knocked off. He took the gloves home, hung them up and tried soccer.

A big, solemn stevedore who occasionally passed the time of day trading lies with Jimmy's father in the furniture store watched the boy one day and asked if he had ever boxed. "He's got legs like trees and he's built sturdy," said the stevedore, a middle-aged man from Liverpool named Charlie Foster. "I've boxed some myself and I could teach him."

Foster, called Pop, had fought in the Boer and Great Wars and had been wounded in both legs. He had boxed in the days of Jim Fitzsimmons and James J. Corbett in a touring circus (he took on all comers, paying a pound for every round the country bumpkins lasted against him). Later he trained and managed fighters in Europe and was a shrewd, sharp, demanding, patient, gentle, honest man in all the years he handled McLarnin.

From the beginning he worked on Jimmy's left hand. He made the youngster—four-foot-six, eighty-five pounds and eleven years old when they started—

do everything with it; he balanced on it, painted houses and fences with it, threw darts and rowed a boat with it, chopped wood, hauled in fish nets and squeezed a sponge ball with it. When he sparred or punched the bag, he concentrated on it. Soon after his twelfth birthday he was matched against a cherub called Clarence Robinson at a military smoker, and came out with a four-round draw. He quit school when he was thirteen, got a job running an elevator for eight dollars a week, and picked up a dollar now and then in amateur bouts. When he was sixteen Foster took him to San Francisco, where he became a professional.

By this time his left hand was passable—fast and fairly accurate. Pop really never was fully satisfied with it, however. Fourteen years after his professional debut McLarnin's left hand won the welterweight championship—he knocked out Young Corbett in the first round without throwing a single right-hand punch. Still, after McLarnin retired, Foster said, "There's just one thing I'm sorry about, Jim. Your left hand—it never did get as good as it should."

McLarnin lived on Foster's World War I pension cheque in San Franscisco, where they cooked meals in their cheap room and went fishing for crabs in a borrowed boat. McLarnin trained in a gym nearby but had difficulty persuading promoters to give him a fight because of his round pink face and wide eyes (until the day he retired, sportswriters called him Baby-Face.)

One afternoon he worked against the welterweight champion of California, Jimmy Duffy, who weighed 145 pounds to McLarnin's 108. Alerted by Foster that a San Francisco promoter named Tommy Simpson was visiting the gym, McLarnin danced and darted and boxed and fled for three rounds, infuriating Duffy but earning a preliminary spot on Simpson's next card. In that first professional fight McLarnin easily handled flyweight Frankie Sands, for which he was paid fifty dollars and earned ten more fights for the same promoter during the next four months. By then his fee was two hundred dollars.

They moved on to Los Angeles. McLarnin won three bouts and was then matched with Fidel La Barba, who had just won an Olympic gold medal in Paris. McLarnin won in four rounds. In a rematch they fought to a draw, revealing such warming skills that they got top billing for a third match at ten rounds. McLarnin won it, earned three thousand dollars and never again fought underneath – his fights thereafter were main events.

He fought all the great ones through the next eleven years. His three fights in New York against Barney Ross for the welterweight championship are remembered as boxing classics, each savage, relentless work for both fighters. All three bouts lasted fifteen rounds – the first in May, 1934, then in September, 1934, and finally in May, 1935. At the peak of the depression 125,000 people paid $525,000 to see the Irish McLarnin against the Jewish Ross; it was an Abie's Irish Rose of the prize ring, and it drove New Yorkers delirious. In the first fight, McLarnin was defending for the first time the championship he had won from Young Corbett. He lost a split decision. He regained the championship in the second fight; again the two judges and the referee split their ballots. Then he lost the third fight and the title, and for a third time the ballots were split. In all three fights, the decision was roundly booed; the fights were so close, and the partiality of the Irish and Jewish fans was so vivid, that no decision could possibly have been popular with everybody.

Demanding of McLarnin's skills, guts and experience as these fights were, they were neither his best nor his most courageous. Pop Foster always insisted McLarnin made the best fight of his life in the fall of 1927. This one was against Kid Kaplan, who had been featherweight champion for two years and was now foraging among the lightweights. He had won eleven straight bouts. McLarnin at this time had turned sour, though still only a boy of nineteen. A growth spurt and a lingering invasion of jaundice had sapped his stamina, producing so many bad fights that west-coast promoters had begun bypassing him. By then he had saved twenty-five thousand dollars and, disgusted, wanted to quit the ring. Foster cajoled patiently, finally suggesting they move east. He bought an old Buick and drove the listless McLarnin to Chicago. Two offers fell through, and then they were offered the rising Kaplan. Foster demurred, wary as always, but desperation outweighed judgment.

Kaplan broke McLarnin's jaw with the first punch of the fight. McLarnin went down for the first time ever, and in his pain and bewilderment lurched upright at the count of four. Through three rounds Kaplan followed him along the ropes, methodically sinking his fists into the mobile punching-bag he pursued. McLarnin vainly tried to cover his unhinged chin with his hands and his welt-ridden ribs and stomach with his elbows. He was knocked down three times.

Between rounds Foster called instructions. After the third, he simply said, "Jimmy, why don't *you* try hitting *him*?" McLarnin began swinging, desperately and at times hopelessly. But slowly his head cleared and his punches grew more accurate. In the eighth round he landed two rights to Kaplan's chin. Kaplan's eyes glazed and McLarnin measured another right as carefully as a tailor cutting cashmere. He knocked Kaplan out.

Three years later, in November, 1930, McLarnin met the fighter he later recalled as the toughest of them all. This was Billy Petrolle, a man who could almost hide behind his own scar tissue, a veteran of 157 fights who was called the Fargo Express. In the first round Petrolle came out of his customary flat-footed crouch and cut McLarnin under the left eye. In the second, McLarnin threw a right at Petrolle's open jaw. When

Petrolle ducked, McLarnin's hand exploded on his head. Pain shot along his arm so harsh that he was blind for many seconds. He had broken his right hand. Petrolle threw a barrage of punches at his chin and he almost went down. But he rallied in the third, jarring Petrolle with his left jab. In the fourth, Petrolle landed a twisting left hook on McLarnin's chin and he went down. He reeled to his feet at the count of nine, and Petrolle hit him, hard, several times. McLarnin crumpled again, laboured back to his feet, and absorbed the cruelest beating he had ever taken. During this round a man named Al Golden, who happened to be a part owner of King's Park race course in Montreal, suffered a fatal heart seizure in the excitement.

In the fifth and sixth rounds, Petrolle worked on McLarnin's ribs and chin. By the seventh, McLarnin's face was mainly lumps and blood. At the end of the round New York's mayor, Jimmy Walker, got hurriedly to his feet and left Madison Square Garden, unable to digest more of the scene. In the eighth Petrolle hammered McLarnin around the ring so remorselessly that the crowd yelled at the referee to stop the fight. He grabbed McLarnin and peered into his face. McLarnin shook him away.

By the ninth round the crowd began to go quite mad; fights broke out all over the Garden. Both fighters *in* the ring were labouring on their feet, Petrolle wearying from delivering so many punches, McLarnin plodding back from every attack. Near the end of the fight they fell into a clinch, leaning on each other's shoulders, eyes closed, gasping. Then they separated, stood toe to toe and swung from the hips, all pretense of defense abandoned. The bell was moments penetrating their clouded minds; they continued to throw punches after it sounded.

Petrolle won a unanimous decision. In a hotel room afterwards McLarnin, both eyes puffed nearly shut, his body racked, turned to Foster. "Well, Pop," he muttered, "I guess that's it."

"We'll see," said Pop. "We'll see."

McLarnin's kidneys bled for three weeks but there was no permanent damage. Six months later he agreed to a rematch.

"Pop, can I beat Petrolle?" he asked.

"If you box him," Foster said. "Not if you slug with him."

Boxing with care and artistry, McLarnin won the decision. Three months later they met again in Yankee Stadium. In the first three rounds McLarnin boxed in the classic mould, jabbing sharply through Petrolle's defense, hooking hard to the body. When Petrolle's guard came down, McLarnin hit him savagely in the head. He beat Petrolle even more grievously, some writers said, than that destructive man had beaten him.

Oh, he had guts, that McLarnin. He had the guts of a bugler. Kipling's bugler.   TRENT FRAYNE

STRENGTH

Was Louis Cyr the strongest man who ever lived? Many Canadians think he was. Others argue that he wasn't even the strongest *Canadian* who ever lived.

Whichever it is, Cyr's name tops a list of athletes whose muscle power has added immeasurably to the colour and achievements of the world of Canadian sport.

Ebullient Nancy McCredie, probably the strongest woman athlete in the free world of the 1960s (*no one* is as strong as Russian women), broke the Canadian shot-put record by ten feet in 1963. She was 17.

Shoulders: the hub of strength

Bobby Hull, the Chicago Black Hawks' "Golden Jet," is so strong he can fend off opposing defensemen with one casually outstretched arm — using the same muscles he throws into forking hay on his Ontario farm.

Size, weight— even shape— have little to do with power

Over the years, three different native sons of Zorra, in Ontario's Oxford County, have become United States senators. Really. But the *real* heroes among Zorra men were these five farmers, the smallest of whom stood 6′1″ and weighed 188. On July 4, 1893, at the Chicago World's Fair, they outpulled teams from Britain, France, Belgium, Germany and the U.S. to become tug-of-war champions of the world.

Pound for pound, Tommy Burns from Hanover, Ontario, may well have been the most powerful boxer who ever lived. At 162, he gave as much as a hundred pounds to his opponents, but from 1901 to 1920 he fought sixty of them and was beaten by only four. From 1906 to 1908, when he lost his title to Jack Johnson, Burns was heavyweight champion of the world — the smallest ever. During his championship days, as when this picture was taken in London (Burns is the man with the velvet collar), he was almost as dapper as he was strong.

There have been stronger discus throwers than
Jackie MacDonald, but none prettier. Jackie was
the belle of the 1954 British Empire Games in
Vancouver, and until Nancy McCredie came along, the
strongest woman athlete in Canada's recent history.
She could lift 205 pounds in barbells. Her
own weight: a trim 150, distributed over 5'10".
Further statistics: 41½, 28, 40.

Budd Schulberg, author of *The Harder They Fall,*
once invested in a big heavyweight himself:
Alex Miteff. Here Miteff is falling appropriately hard
under the fists of George Chuvalo, Canada's fine,
strong (if unpolished) champion of the 1960s.

This muscular Montreal policeman,
Etienne Desmarteau, was one of
Canada's first Olympic champions —
winner of the hammer-throw at
St. Louis in 1904.

Doug Hepburn of Vancouver, who'd conquered
the handicap of the crippled leg he was born with,
never won an Olympic medal. By 1952, interest
in weightlifting was so low in Canada he wasn't
even sent to the Helsinki Olympics. But the
next year, Hepburn and his friends raised $1,400
themselves to send him to Stockholm, where, at the
age of 26, he outlifted the Olympic champion and
everyone else to win for himself officially Louis Cyr's
old unofficial title of World's Strongest Man.

If Cyr wasn't strongest, maybe Hepburn was

LOUIS CYR

An elephant among strongmen

He died in 1912, at forty-nine. His early death, some men said, was a direct result of the voracious way he had charged through life. His appetites were as enormous as his energies. For the last fifteen years of his life he was less than well, plagued by heart trouble and asthma, unable to use a bed, taking his rest in a Morris chair. Toward the end his diet consisted solely of milk. But at his peak, in the young years of Canadian Confederation, Louis Cyr was the strongest man in the world, some say the strongest who ever lived – a folk hero.

In private, he longed to be a musician. "During my moments of leisure," he once reminisced, "I would scratch away at the violin. Ernest Lavigne of Montreal, who ran a music store, knew about my love for the instrument and made me a present of one, which I always carried with me. Later he gave me lessons at his home and I got so I could play fairly well. The moments I had with the violin were among the happiest in my memory." But in public there was nothing gentle or dainty or stylish about him. He was simply a very strong man. At twenty-nine, when he was at the peak of his career, he weighed three hundred and fifteen pounds, though he stood an inch and a half under six feet. His thighs were as thick as many men's waists, thirty-three inches around. His chest, relaxed, was sixty inches; he could expand it another seven. His waist measurement was forty-seven inches. He was twenty-eight inches around the calf, twenty-two and a half around the biceps, nineteen and a half around the forearm, and at times it must have seemed that there was nothing in the world he could not lift.

Today, it is impossible to say what the limits of Cyr's prodigious strength might have been. For one thing, as Andy O'Brien, the sports editor of *Weekend* magazine, who has made himself something of an authority on Cyriana, has commented, "Canadian reporters became fanatical fans, oozing with superlatives if Louis hoisted anything heavier than a five-cent schooner of beer." For another, many of Cyr's greatest feats were accomplished in two-man competitions. And Cyr, like that other great Canadian champion of the nineteenth century, Ned Hanlan, usually competed just hard enough to win: when he had bettered his opponent, he stopped. Victory was more important to him than any records he might have set.

Nevertheless, there are many accounts of specific Cyr lifts that – incredible as some of them may seem – were recorded by independent and reliable witnesses. The lift that was, and has remained, his trademark involved raising with his back and shoulders a platform loaded with many hundred pounds of weight. His first record of this sort was set at Berthierville, Quebec, in 1888. There, the platform carried a load of pig-iron weighing 3,526 pounds. Later he took to making up his load of big men from the audience. In Boston he stood eighteen fat men on his platform, and lifted them all. Their total weight was 4,300 pounds. The greatest lift of this kind he ever made was at Sohmer Park in Montreal in 1894 before a crowd of more than ten thousand. The total weight of his living burden was 4,562 pounds. There is no record of how many men it was composed of.

Weight-lifting was not recognized at the Olympics until 1920, eight years after Cyr's death; there are few ways to measure his achievements against the records of more modern weight-lifters, who work to rigid rules. Where comparisons are in order, Cyr is not triumphant. One man whose record shines brighter is Doug Hepburn, the Vancouver athlete who, in the 1950s, succeeded officially to the title that Cyr held unofficially, world's strongest man.

In London, in 1892, Cyr was reported to have

stood "military-like" while raising a 301-pound bar-bell with two hands from the floor to his shoulder and "pressing it slowly overhead." In essence, this is the modern "press." In Stockholm, in 1953, Hepburn pressed a record 369 pounds on his way to the world's championship. In the same tournament, Hepburn "snatched" – lifted overhead in one movement – 363 pounds. In New York, in 1896, Cyr, with a similar action ("He lifted the barbell in a rush from the floor without squatting or even dipping, one heave from the floor to full arms' length"), managed only 347 pounds. But few weight-lifting experts would maintain that even Hepburn would have been Cyr's match if they had met on equal terms; in the six decades between their individual reigns as the world's strongest man, a great deal of knowledge about diet, training and tech-nique was added to their sport.

Further, Cyr's achievements were often part of a long evening's show. Before he got to the equivalent of the modern snatch or press he might have run through much of his repertoire of stunts. At this kind of stunt – admittedly almost as much show business as sport – Cyr has never really been equalled. He could raise 987 pounds with one hand. On one occasion he lifted, one-handed, a barrel of wet sand weighing 432 pounds and put it on his shoulder. In several different exhibitions he lifted more than 550 pounds with one *finger*. Still another of his favourite stunts – and nearly as distinct a trademark as his celebrated platform lifts – was to restrain horses by strength alone. On a tour of England he was once challenged by the Marquis of Queensberry to hold two of the Marquis's best driving horses. Cyr hitched one to each arm, then gave the word to have them pull in opposite directions. Neither could budge. The Marquis, son of the man who had encoded the rules of boxing, offered Cyr his choice of either animal as a reward. For years after-ward, Cyr sitting proudly behind his high-bred English driving horse was a familiar sight on the streets of Montreal. Later, at Montreal's Sohmer Park, Cyr capped even this feat by holding two teams of Quebec farm horses – four horses in all – at a standstill. It would be hard to argue against the claim that has often been made: that Canada's Louis Cyr was the strongest man who ever lived.

Cyr's story has the dimensions of legend from its outset. He was born in 1863, the oldest son among the seventeen children of a farmer from St. Cyprien de Napierville, Quebec. His father, according to contem-porary reports, was a man of normal build and strength. Louis inherited his power from his mother. Mme. Cyr was over six feet tall and weighed close to two hundred and seventy pounds. Around St. Cyprien she was known to be able to climb a barn ladder carry-ing a hundred-pound grain sack on each shoulder. Louis weighed eighteen pounds when he was born.

At twelve he left school to help his family. Ac-counts of how his extraordinary strength first came to be noticed have been clouded by time and by the imagination of his local biographers, so that it is now hard to sort out fact from legend. Robert L. Gowe, in an authoritative article published in 1963, reports that young Cyr got his first job at twelve when he dis-covered a neighbouring farmer lying injured on a country road. Cyr, this story has it, lifted the man to his shoulder and carried him the two miles to his home. The farmer hired him on the spot. Another version has Cyr coming upon a broken-down, heavily loaded wagon, and lifting *it* bodily from the ditch. In any case, before he reached his mid-teens young Louis was the talk of the *paysage*.

When Cyr was fifteen his family moved to Lowell, Massachusetts. He worked at odd jobs for a while, and – again according to legend – he was fired from a textile mill when he was seventeen; the other workers persisted in watching him perform his feats of strength when they should have been working. In his late teens Cyr met and fell in love with a tiny French-Canadian girl whose family had also moved to New England, and in 1882 they were married. The young Mme. Cyr was a startling contrast to her amazonian mother-in-law: she weighed slightly over a hundred pounds. Her husband by this time outweighed her by a hundred and fifty pounds.

Cyr was easily the strongman champion of Lowell, but he was still having difficulty earning a living. After the birth of his only daughter, christened Emiliana, he moved with his family to Montreal, where he joined the police. The beat he was assigned to was in the tough Sainte Cunegonde district, and his strength soon became known and feared along Sainte Cunegonde's *rues*. His fame spread quickly. "He figured," an anony-mous reporter on the Montreal *Star* once wrote of Cyr, "in several noted captures of criminals and stick-up men. Early one morning, he walked into his station and handed over three husky toughs whom he had arrested in the downtown section. At first the arrested ones had endeavoured to put up a fight, but Cyr, taking one under each arm and carrying the other in a vice-like grip in front of him, marched off to the station with all three prisoners off the ground."

It was this remarkable arrest that led, eventually, to Cyr's worldwide fame. The news of it spread to the New York papers, and there caught the attention of the famous editor of the old *Police Gazette*, R. A. K. Fox. Fox wrote to Cyr, which began an association that was to have lasting effects on Cyr's career. Through Fox's interest a meeting was arranged in Lowell between Cyr and the man who was then the strongman champion of the United States, Richard Pennell. Cyr, setting the pattern he was to follow so often, matched each of Pennell's feats and then topped them, but appeared not to extend himself.

As a mature man and a champion strongman, Cyr was soon a famous figure in Montreal – nearly as famous for his appetites as for his strength; a biographer has guessed that he averaged twelve pounds of meat a day. One of his most celebrated abilities was to consume a whole suckling pig in twenty minutes. His friends included some of the most famous people of his time. One of them was the gigantic priest who helped to settle so many of French Canada's northern "colonies," the Curé Labelle, and one of the most popular sights in Montreal was Cyr and the curé putting on what in effect were eating contests in one of the restaurants near the old court house.

Another of Cyr's friends was John L. Sullivan, the heavyweight champion. Robert L. Gowe says the meeting of these two titans came about this way: Sullivan entered a bar in Boston and ordered drinks for everyone, as was his custom. Cyr, who was in the bar but who, for all his appetite for food, seldom drank, declined the offer. Sullivan, enraged, tried to flatten Cyr with a punch to the midsection. Cyr didn't flinch. "Who are you, anyway?" Sullivan said. "I am Louis Cyr, the strongest man in the world, and I am pleased to meet the greatest fighter in the world," Cyr replied, and the two began their friendship. Much later, Cyr was to write: "John was a joyous friend, always ready for anything. I saw him throw money 'out of the window' in hundred-dollar bills, spending huge sums foolishly without thought of tomorrow. He drank a little too much and I was always afraid of accidents when I was with him. Nevertheless, John L. was a great man in many ways."

Cyr, apparently, was nearly as sensible with his money as Sullivan was profligate with his. Through Fox's guidance, he was the first great strongman ever properly to exploit his skills and, over the years, he was able to save a sizeable nest-egg.

In 1892, when he was twenty-nine, Cyr began his tour of England and Europe. Fox put up a standing offer of a thousand pounds sterling that no one could better his champion's feats, and throughout his triumphant tour no one dared even challenge Cyr.

The closest anyone ever came to winning Fox's money was in April, 1896, long after Cyr had returned to America. The challenger was a Swede, August W. Johnson. Johnson and Cyr met in Chicago and the stakes were a thousand-dollar wager and the title of world champion. The match began at ten o'clock in the evening. It consisted of lifting barrels, holding out dumb-bells, lifting weights from the shoulder— virtually every act of sheer strength short of Cyr's special stunts with living men or horses. The two were nearly equal, and there was no decision until one o'clock in the morning. Then, pound by pound, Cyr's margin in the total they had lifted reached two hundred pounds. "I have conquered strongmen all over the world," Johnson is reported to have said, "but this time I have met an elephant."

The elephant was to reign over the world's strongmen until only five years before his death. For a time he operated a restaurant in the Sainte Cunegonde area where he had first become famous as a policeman. Over another period, lacking any real competition for two-man matches, he was a star attraction of the Ringling Bros., Barnum and Bailey Circus, billed as "The World's Strongest Man."

At forty-four Cyr was still able to outlift two great French-Canadian pretenders to his throne, Hector Decarie and Horace Barre. For a while, during his match with Decarie, Cyr appeared to be in trouble. He declined to match Decarie's best one-hand lift. But Cyr still had his specialty in reserve. Two horses, weighing a total of nearly three thousand pounds, were placed on a special platform. Decarie, the challenger, strained but failed to budge it. Then Cyr, with a great explosion of energy, shouldered it off the ground and held it in the air for a full minute.

His victory over Decarie was to be his last public appearance. His health was failing too fast, drained by his appetites and his exploits. No descendants survive. His daughter Emiliana, who might have carried on the line just as Cyr's mother had—Emiliana once lifted four hundred and fifty pounds—entered a convent in her twenties.

PETER GZOWSKI

Strong? He once lifted 550 pounds with one finger.

109

The royal spectacle of Canadian sport, the Queen's Plate, is a great day even for losers.

SHOWMANSHIP

To fill the standing room, it's not enough to be good at the game. Colour's what counts.

Sometimes the crowds, caught up in a vague momentary excitement, are far more colourful than
the athletes they idolize. On this day in Vancouver the lampooned Lions finally
turned ferocious — after a decade of degradation they made the western football playoffs.
Chinatown went daffy over the new heroes, and so did people everywhere in the city, most of
whom didn't know a quarterback from twenty-five cents in change.

Great showmen clearly stamp the games they play — or just watch

Showboating isn't showmanship, especially in golf where there's usually a trick shooter
who can't sink a three-footer for money but can pierce an arrow for kicks. Again, though,
class and colour are the unbeatable ingredients, and among the very few Canadians
who combined both was George S. Lyon, the (inevitably) Grand Old Man of Canadian golf, who
won the Olympic gold medal for golf at St. Louis in 1904, when there were such things.

Curiously, Conn Smythe, an acerbic man of rigid discipline, was sufficiently flamboyant to sell hockey in the big eastern arenas. He walked the boards to get at referees and baited fans derisively. He was a dressing-room martinet. But the customers flocked to the sound of his flute in Boston and New York and the rest of the NHL towns. His game became one of the big professional sports, and the rink he built grew into a national institution. (Photo shows Smythe on the night Maple Leaf Gardens opened.)
Some of his players cursed him, but they became champions.

Every move Fred (Cyclone) Taylor made was a picture of controlled fury. One move especially left his mark on the game: he was the first man to skate backwards — fast.

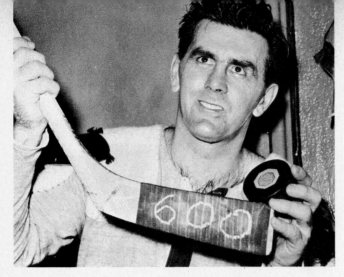

When Maurice Richard twirled and twisted
in front of the enemy's net, wild horses couldn't
contain him — or the fans. When the
Rocket glared, the crowds came up wild-eyed too.

Colour can be natural—or manufactured like bubble-gum

Don Jackson, an Olympic champion who was perhaps
the finest of all Canadian figure skaters, had
the verve and dash of a drowsy caterpillar.
But curvy cutey-pies were festooned around him
like excelsior when he turned pro with the
Ice Capades, and they added colour to his class.

Sometimes a nickname will put the facade of
showmanship around a journeyman. Bernard Geoffrion
was a blocky brooding little guy at right wing for
the Canadiens. When someone translated his hard shot
into the appellation Boom Boom, Geoffrion became a
man apart, even opened a bar proclaiming the proclivity.

Barry

Oliver

Smith

Hitchm.

Jackson

Clapper

Stewart

Beatty

KING CLANCY

The leprechaun on
the rubbing table

It has been said of King Clancy that he was born drunk, a fiendish accusation to bring against a lifelong teetotaller but, still, as plausible an explanation as any for the irrepressible elan of a leprechaun who bounded into hockey's Hall of Fame while actually enjoying himself. Canada produced her share of athletic heroes in her first century but Clancy was unfettered *and* accomplished, and this made him one of a kind, or close to it.

Clancy oozed colour and flair; everything he did, he did with the joyous abandon of a kid in a pond on a hot summer day. By contrast, there was nothing about the business silhouettes of most of our gristly nonpareils to suggest they were enjoying their work. Syl Apps and Milt Schmidt and Frank Boucher and Jean Beliveau, among the great centres, displayed the colour of dress-shirts at a Stanley Cup dinner in leading their playmates to unexpected plateaus, and Joe Krol and Russ Jackson, the best of the Canadian-born quarterbacks, were aloof and calculating precisionists in running their offenses. Stan Leonard and Sandy Somerville toured the greatest golf courses, often with unmatched success but always as though their feet hurt. Percy Williams ran to lasting fame wearing the expression of a lady who had rent her girdle, and Barbara Ann Scott's pop-eyed smile was as fixed and unwarmed as a bayonet. Maybe Gordie Howe enjoyed his work, but if he did it was a secret he shared only with his friends and relatives. On the ice he was an absolute marvel at all of hockey's myriad requirements, including hemstitching, but he brought off his feats in a sort of *Who, me?* manner that closed the door on showmanship. Conn Smythe and Rocket Richard had it by the bucket, but Smythe's fulminations were sardonic and unleavened by wit, and Richard's exploits were imprinted with the pitiless efficiency of a hangman.

That leaves Clancy. Francis Michael Clancy was a rowdy hockey player and rowdier rascal who knew all the angles and invented a few that would have confounded Euclid. Then, as an NHL referee for eleven years, he continued to get in the last word with a tongue that once, implausibly, won a vital playoff for the Toronto Maple Leafs. Clancy was a fox terrier among defensemen, weighing 157 pounds through his

best years. He yapped and scrapped and inspired his mates with his absolute antipathy for defeat. He played for nine seasons with the old Ottawa Senators, hockey's greatest team in the early 1920s, and then he was sold for thirty-five thousand dollars to Toronto. It was an unprecedented sum and one made even more conspicuous by the fact that Conn Smythe paid it in the early years of the depression, when he was already mortgaged to his eyeballs in building Maple Leaf Gardens. Clancy was worth every quarter of the money for six seasons more; he was named on all-star teams four times, which doesn't properly reflect his ability because the first all-star teams did not come along until the 1930-31 season, Clancy's eleventh in the big time.

There was no moment of it that he didn't enjoy. His philosophy was that of another bon vivant of the athletic half-world, Walter Hagen. "You only pass this way once," Hagen used to say, "so you may as well smell the flowers." Clancy smelled them just this side of constantly. He had a way of relaxing such great puck manipulators as Charlie Conacher, Busher Jackson and Red Horner and sending them onto the ice with confidence, making impassioned speeches in the dressing room while standing high on a rubbing table, often stark naked, waving his arms, a marvellously comic figure. Moments before the team moved out of its dressing quarters for the first game of the 1932 final against the New York Rangers, Clancy noticed that the players were taut and nervous. They were underdogs against the great Ranger team of Boucher, the Cooks, Taffy Abel and Ching Johnson.

"Well," cried the King, leaping onto the rubbing table, sartorially impeccable in his jock strap, "I have great confidence in our defense but I fear for the forwards. I don't think the shooting will be sharp. You big bastards have the look of lambs. I'll show you what I expect."

He hopped down into a room now quiet. The grim players, distracted, turned to watch as Clancy wandered over to a pile of hockey sticks, selected one, tossed a puck on the floor, and took aim at an alarm clock that the trainer, Tim Daly, kept on a stool. The players guffawed and called insults; Clancy was a bad bet to hit the clock in a dozen tries.

He fired the puck. It smashed the clock, spilling glass and works around the room. Clancy casually replaced the stick in the pile, strolled nonchalantly to his locker and began climbing into his gear. The room exploded in laughter and coarse profanity. Charlie Conacher rolled on the floor in delight. Then he scored three goals as the Leafs won, six to two, and went on to win the series in straight games for their first Stanley Cup victory.

Nobody could long stay tense when Clancy was around. At the University Club in Boston, where the Leafs stayed, he and Conacher and Eddie Convey decided one day to swim in the club's pool after lunch.

Oh, that Clancy! Here was a sweaty personification of showmanship and class. The essence of King: he never changed his style.

Before the meal Clancy overheard the other two plot to trap him beside the pool and throw him in, fully clothed. Later he excused himself from the table, ostensibly to go to the men's room. Instead he sped to Convey's room where he changed into one of Eddie's suits. At the pool, he fought in mock alarm as the other two grabbed him to throw him into the water. Finally he gave in. They were hysterical as he sputtered and snorted, climbed from the water, and turned out the dripping pockets.

"You're a damn fool, Convey," he said in wounded tones, removing letters and papers from the inside pocket of Convey's coat. "All this crap in *your* pockets could of drowned me."

Of course, the Leafs didn't always win during Clancy's years with them, but they never lost a game in which he gave up. Smythe once recalled entering the Toronto dressing room after New York had won the last game of the 1933 Stanley Cup final, one to nothing after seven minutes and thirty-three seconds of overtime. There was Clancy, naked and in his customary belligerent stance on the rubbing table, telling the players they had given their best shot, so why brood? That was the spring in which little Ken Doraty's unforgettable goal eliminated Boston for the Leafs in the first round of the playoffs, producing a one to nothing win after one hundred and four minutes and forty-six seconds of *overtime* in the fifth and deciding game. Then they had departed immediately on the waiting overnight train for New York to open the Stanley Cup final, actually on the night of the morning they had eliminated Boston an hour or so after midnight. They lost that night, five to one, a disadvantage they never overcame as the series progressed. The Boston win, according to Clancy, had made the Leafs "too pooped and too laxadaisical (*sic*)."

Now Clancy spotted Smythe entering the dressing room and called to him from his usual dais, the rubbing table. "It was my fault, Mr. Smythe," he declared solemnly. "They never should have scored that goal."

"Your fault," cried Smythe, incredulous. "You weren't even on the ice."

"It was my team," said Clancy with dignity, revealing the essence of Clancy.

Clancy was a great natural athlete as a boy in Ottawa, where he was born in February, 1902; a star at lacrosse, football, baseball and hockey. When his pants grew long he continued to play hockey for reasons quite unmercenary. "It was the game I liked most," he noted once, "or I wouldn't have played it." In later years he never haggled over his professional pay and he was never a holdout. Negotiations with Smythe lasted exactly four sentences each autumn.

"How much do you want?" Smythe would say.

"How much you givin' me?" Clancy would reply.

"How about such-and-such?"

"That's fine with me."

In those depression times the figure was usually between five and seven thousand dollars a season. Clancy probably invented the cliché, "Imagine being paid to play the game you love." God knows he uttered it often enough. He took the same attitude to refereeing. In eleven years his top fee was eight thousand dollars, and he really didn't need the work. He and two uncles, who revelled in the names Pat and Mike O'Leary, owned a thriving road-construction company in Ottawa, which Clancy took over when his uncles died in the early 1960s, both in their eighties.

"I sometimes used to wish I'd been a referee all my life instead of just part of it," Clancy said one time. "I had more fun bein' a referee."

He carried on a constant stream of chatter with the players. Once, he penalized his old teammate Bob Davidson of Toronto during a frantic moment in a playoff game in Boston. Davidson was incensed.

"Dammit to hell, King," Davidson ranted, "You used to do that yourself."

"I know," Clancy replied civilly, "but I never used to get caught."

Babe Pratt, a big, fun-loving defenseman, is the only player who ever got the last word on Clancy. It happened in Detroit in the seventh game of the 1945 final when Toronto, hard-pressed, was drawing penalty after penalty from Clancy. Once, with a man off, Pratt lumbered down the ice with the puck and lobbed it into the Detroit end to relieve the pressure momentarily. As he turned back to his defense position Pratt collided with Clancy, knocking the referee to the ice. Clancy thought it might have been deliberate but he wasn't sure.

"Pratt, you big bum, I'd like to be playin' against you tonight," he grated.

Pratt stared wide-eyed at the penalty box. "Well," he inquired, "ain't you?"

Clancy rarely lost his sense of humour, even when the packed rinks blistered his ears with abuse. After one such night in Madison Square Garden, where he and Rabbit McVeigh had worked as linesmen with referee Mickey Ion, the three of them were walking across Eighth Avenue in a howling cold rainstorm. As they hunkered along, Ion stopped suddenly, bent down near the gutter and picked up a piece of paper. It was a ten-dollar bill.

"Fer the luv of gawd," said Clancy reverently, peering over Ion's shoulder at the money. "Sixteen thousand of them nuts have crossed this street – and they call referees blind!"

As a player Clancy never won a fight, but he started a hundred. "Nothing relaxes the boys like a good fight," he used to say. "I'd start 'em just to get fellahs like Conacher and Horner to relax."

Years later, when Clancy was assistant to George Imlach, the coach and general manager of the Leafs, he held the same theory. In the spring of 1965 Toronto came up to the sixth game trailing by one game, and that afternoon Clancy was having lunch with a friend.

"They're all tied up in knots," Clancy complained of the Leaf players. "If I was playin' tonight I'd pick me a fight with that big bastard Beliveau in the first minute. They'd all come in to save me and they'd be loose as a goose."

He was asked why he didn't instruct a Leaf player to start a fight.

"Aw, you can't *tell* a guy to do it," said Clancy. "He's got to *feel* it."

Clancy's teammates knew he couldn't lick his lips, so they loved his audacity. Once in Montreal he got embroiled with a big fellow named Harold Starr, a Maroons defenseman who had been a professional wrestler. Charlie Conacher and Busher Jackson determined that this was one fight Clancy was going to win. They skated to the untidy mound that was Clancy on the bottom and Starr on top, rolled them over and put Clancy on top of Starr. Then they skated away. They had gone only a few strides when Jackson looked back. "Don't look now, Chuck," he said to Conacher, "but Starr's on top again."

The sheer joy of contact exhilarated Clancy, who never was vicious or crude or furtive, and the size of his opponent was mostly incidental. He once took on Nels Stewart, of all people, a burly Maroon of the classical school who always removed his gloves before knocking somebody cross-eyed. Stewart took a swipe at Clancy, missed, and hammered his hand into the boards. When Clancy saw Stewart's face contort he stopped scrambling and took hold of Stewart's thumb, which had been knocked out of joint by the boards. He pulled on it, restoring it to normal, and enquired if it felt all right. When Stewart nodded, Clancy belted him across the nose and fled to the Leaf bench, laughing fiendishly.

For all the fun, though, winning meant as much to Clancy – winning *and* fun, not one without the other. His classic contribution, the unforgettable moment, arrived on the night of March 26, 1936, when the Leafs were in desperate shape against the Bruins. This was one of the good Boston teams, with the fearsome Eddie Shore and Babe Siebert, a redoubtable defense pair, Tiny Thompson the goalkeeper, and the excellent forward line of Cooney Weiland, Dit Clapper and Red Beattie, the leftwinger who led the Boston scorers that season. The series involved total goals over two games. The Bruins won the first game in Boston, three to nothing, and scored again in the first period of the Toronto game.

Thus the Leafs were trailing four to nothing as they clomped between periods to their dressing quarters, in which, incidentally, they were forbidden to smoke. The players' lavatory cubicle was just off the main room, and when Charlie Conacher stole in for a few puffs he found Clancy already sitting on the toilet, staring thoughtfully at smoke rings.

"Get up," grunted Conacher.

"Get up? What the hell do you mean, get up?" piped Clancy in his high, strained brogue. "I'll not be gettin' up fer a son of a bitch who's waltzin' around like you are tonight."

Clancy had hit a sore spot with Conacher. He was one of the league's great scorers but he had scarcely caused a draft around Tiny Thompson in four periods of the series. The main reason was that Red Beattie was shadowing him every stride he was on the ice. Conacher reminded Clancy of this.

"Well, now, sit down," said Clancy, getting to his feet and passing the cigaret to Conacher. When the big man sat down, the little man climbed into his lap and placed a conspiratorial hand on his shoulder.

"Why don't you give it to him good?" Clancy asked. "Why don't you belt him once and for all and be rid of the sneaky bastard?"

"And get a penalty," said Conacher. "What good would I be sitting there?"

"So what's a penalty?" asked Clancy. "Look, I'll get the puck and I'll wait till Beattie's right beside you. Then I'll pass it to you and when Beattie's reachin' fer the puck, give him a belt he'll never forget."

That is what happened. Conacher jammed his hard-fibre elbow pad into Beattie's face, and the referee missed it. A few minutes later Clancy tripped the Boston mainspring, Shore, and the referee, Odie Cleghorn, missed that one, too. Shore was livid, protesting vainly to Cleghorn. Clancy skated up and needled Shore, to make matters worse.

"The man's blind, Eddie," he cooed. "Yer bein' robbed, man, surer than hell. And he blew that one on Beattie, too."

And then Red Horner, standing on the edge of the goal crease, deflected a shot from Art Jackson past Thompson for a Leaf goal. The Bruins surrounded Cleghorn, insisting Horner was standing inside the crease, making the shot illegal. Shore argued bitterly, and then Clancy floated by.

"Gawd, Eddie, what a terrible decision. Yer bein' robbed, man; yer bein' robbed blind."

Incensed even without Clancy's needle and wild with it, Shore fired the puck at Cleghorn, and it whacked him on the buttock as he turned from the protesting players. He showed admirable restraint in assessing Shore only a minor penalty, but this drove Shore to distraction. He picked up the puck and flung it angrily into the crowd, and Cleghorn added a ten-minute misconduct penalty. Thus Boston's leading player spent the next twelve minutes sitting in helpless wrath. The turn of events demoralized the Bruins and served as adrenalin for the Leafs, who scored four goals while Shore was away and went on to rout the Bruins eight to three, which gave them the series, eight to six.

Clancy, laughing like a hyena, surely is the only hockey player in the history of the NHL who ever talked the enemy into elimination. TRENT FRAYNE

The year was 1908. The place, Toronto Bay. The sport, iceboating – and *everybody* did it.

Epilogue: The changing styles of watching and playing   PETER GZOWSKI

In a sense, the history of sport in Canada is coming full cycle. The pioneers who first settled the cold, open spaces of the country had little enough time to indulge in games, and no time to watch other people playing. When their search for relaxation turned to athletics it was the athletics of participation. But by the year of Confederation, Canadians had developed a hearty interest in spectator sports. One of the special activities that marked July first, 1867, in Toronto was a match between the Toronto Lacrosse Club and the Six Nations Indians – won, for what it signifies, by the Indians, three goals to none. And for much of the first century of its existence, Canada, like most other countries of the Western world, was a nation more devoted to watching games than to playing them.

The interest in spectator sport reached its peak in the two decades following World War II – the era that Herbert Warren Wind has christened the Gilded Age of Sport. With talented businessmen directing the fortunes of the various professional leagues, and the world's most extended television network delivering the contests and results into millions of new fans' living-rooms, sports became as profitable to produce as they were enjoyable to follow. It was the age of the mass market, of spectacles engineered for giant audiences and – for the athletes – it was the age of high salaries, generous pensions and lucrative commercial endorsements, truly the Gilded Age. But by the end of the second postwar decade, the gilt was wearing thin.

The National Hockey League – that culmination of both enterprise and interest in Canadian sport – remains, in the middle 1960s, in a state of health. With the prospect of expansion into more U.S. cities and onto American television, it has on the surface an even healthier future. But perhaps the most significant fact about the NHL's health is that it makes it almost unique among professional sports organizations that depend to a large extent on the support of Canadian spectators, as opposed to participants, for their support.

Baseball, to all intents, is a dead item in Canada. One Triple-A team, a training school for the Boston Red Sox, lives a precarious and subsidized life in Toronto, nurtured by a small band of fanatically optimistic executives. When the team arrived from spring training in April, 1965, only four players had ever been to Canada before. Boxing is staggering against the ropes. There is scarcely a fan in the nation who could so much as name the Canadian middleweight

Portrait of a man and an era: when
Rocket Richard was at his peak (here, a
minor riot at Detroit Olympia in '56)
he *lived* hockey. The game was that serious.

champion. Even football seems to have reached the end of the boom that started in western Canada in the 1930s and spread east. In the very cities that were the underpinning of football's rise to national prominence – cities like Edmonton and Regina – teams are losing money; the recovery from the postwar football fever that swept across Canada may well be following the same route as the disease. Soccer and lacrosse remain minority sports, followed by fans with special, often ethnic, interests in special teams. Only golf, with a purse of one hundred thousand dollars for the 1965 Canadian Open, and a world tournament scheduled for Toronto in 1967, seems, along with hockey, to be going forward, and no golfer can yet make his living playing solely before Canadian crowds. (Horse-racing, of course, is undergoing a spectacular boom of its own, with horses running for record purses before record crowds who bet record amounts of money. And this boom, which started with the advent of E. P. Taylor as breeder and executive, has been accelerated by the success of Northern Dancer. But as a *spectator* sport? Racing, it happens to be the opinion of both the authors of this book, one professionally, one amateurishly, is one of the sporting world's most attractive and absorbing spectacles. But even E. P. Taylor must shudder at the thought of how many people would watch either thoroughbreds or standardbreds if they were not allowed to participate by betting.)

If trends in spectator sports in Canada reflect trends in the United States to the degree most Canadian social habits are presumed to, there is little cause for hope among the promoters. In the U.S., according to the magazine *Sports Illustrated*, even National League football – the great success story of the Gilded Age of Sport – is falling from the heights of fashion. Baseball, the Americans' no-longer national pastime, is looking desperately for new markets, although neither of the two major leagues yet seems to be looking seriously in the direction of Canada.

But as the spectator sports decline, the interest in participant sports is rising. As a nation, we seem to be turning back to the traditions of the first settlers; instead of watching, we are playing.

From the grandstands and arenas of the cities we are turning – or returning – to the hills and lakes of the countryside. In 1965 more Canadians were engaging in more sports than ever before, and their interests ranged from playing volleyball on Vancouver Island to skin-diving off Newfoundland. We now spend more than six hundred million dollars a year on sports equipment – aside from boats – and the list of activities we use that equipment for is almost endless; sky-diving, bobsledding, mountain-climbing, handball, squash, polo, *bocce* – there is a sport for everyone, and, it must sometimes seem to people lined up to use some of our crowded facilities, nearly everyone is out trying to find his own. Curling is so popular that it may soon rival hockey as our true national game. Golf courses ring all our major cities like giant lawns; there are more than ninety within reach of Toronto alone. Bodies of water from Wascana Lake in Regina to Montreal's Lachine canal are stippled with the flotillas of weekend yachtsmen. Few autumn meadows escape the hunter's tread.

Most of the new impetus for amateur, participant sport has sprung directly from a phenomenon that has affected most of the prosperous Western world. We are in a new age of leisure everywhere, nearly everyone has more money to spend and more free time to spend it in. In Canada there have been some special conditions; we have been lucky in the resources we have been able to turn to, in the unspoiled land we have been able to turn into easily accessible golf courses, and in the clean, calm water that is still available for boating. Partly for these reasons, one of the most pleasant aspects of our national return to participant sports is our own rediscovery of Canada.

The sport that provides the clearest example of what is happening across the whole sporting horizon is skiing. In the last decade of Canada's first century skiing has attracted an increase of interest that is, as the sportswriters say, phenomenal. As recently as 1950 the resort area around Collingwood, Ontario, to take one example, counted itself lucky to get five hundred skiers on a weekend. In 1965 it counted itself miserable if it didn't get at least five thousand, and sometimes it got twice that. One hundred and twenty-five thousand people went skiing in the Laurentian hills of Quebec in 1950. In 1965 the number was three hundred and fifty thousand. The proportions are at least as impressive at every ski resort in Canada.

The new skiers are people who, only a few years ago, would have spent those weekend sporting hours in front of a television set, watching someone else perform. But now the first excitement of televised sports is wearing off. Too many of the professional leagues seem to be repeating their routines, with only the casts changed. The skiers have found the money, the time and the urge to go out and try something for themselves. In the process they are discovering, along with the pleasures of their chosen sport, some of the pleasures of Canada. Skiing has also, as it happens, begun to produce the kind of champion we may expect to see emerge in more and more sports, as Canadians both widen and specialize their sporting interests. The most recent example, as this is written, is Nancy Greene, a young British Columbian who, in the winter of 1964-65, established herself as the best woman skier in North America.

Portrait of a new man and a new era:
Bobby Hull, the superstar of the later 1960s,
plays hockey for pay *and* fun. Off
season; he forgets it and gets his kicks from
things like speedboating and fishing.

But to find a clear symbol of the new age of amateurism in Canadian sport it is necessary to look no farther than that most Canadian (still) of games, hockey. Almost from the beginning, there has been one dominant player in the National Hockey League. The most recent of these men is Bobby Hull, of the Chicago Black Hawks. Hull, in the middle 1960s, is indisputably the finest player active in the game. It is no precedent to see in his particular approach to hockey a symbol for our whole approach to sport. Over the years, the men who have dominated hockey have all tended to represent their own periods. And to understand clearly what aspects of our changing attitudes Hull represents – as well as to end this book on an appropriate note – it is worth taking a close look, not only at Hull, but at the context into which he fits.

The NHL was founded at the precise half-way point of Canada's first century of sport, in 1917. It did not begin to assume its modern form until well into the 1920s, the period that, in sports, is known as the Golden Age. Boston, the first U.S. city to have an NHL franchise, entered in 1924; New York in 1925; Chicago and Detroit in 1926. The man who typified the Golden Age and dominated hockey was, of course, Howie Morenz, of the Montreal Canadiens. Morenz came into the National League in 1923, and the speed and excitement of his headlong rushes had a direct effect on the league's expansion. Tex Rickard, for instance, the promoter who helped establish the New York (Tex's) Rangers, always said his interest in hockey had begun at the precise instant he first saw Morenz play. And nearly all the other new clubs of the NHL's great period of growth were influenced in one way or another by Morenz and Montreal. Morenz was a typical hero of the frenzied Golden Age, colourful and glamorous, an explosive skater and a burning competitor. Hockey, the free-wheeling hockey of the 1920s and 1930s, was his life, and the sports-happy crowds of the day thronged to see him play and live it. After a loss he would often walk the streets for hours. One Montreal writer has recalled being awakened by Morenz in a Boston hotel room at six in the morning after the Canadiens had lost an overtime playoff game to the Bruins. The winning goal had been scored by Morenz's check and, at dawn, Morenz was still sobbing in frustration.

Morenz died in 1937 – the result, some say, of a broken heart caused by the way his beloved Canadiens had rejected him. His successor, Maurice Richard, emerged as a hockey star in the season of 1943-44, when he scored thirty-two of the 544 goals he was to amass before his retirement. From that year until 1947 there was never a season in which Richard failed to score at least twenty goals. And he, in his turn, typified the Gilded Age of Sport, the second and even more prosperous age of the superstars. Richard was a magnetic performer, as totally dedicated to his game as Morenz; everything he did – from the games he pur-

sued between hockey seasons to his choice of what to eat for breakfast – was aimed at improving his ability to play hockey. The first impression he left on anyone who met him during his prime was the fierce blaze of his eyes, and his temper was never far from detonation.

Richard stayed in the NHL until 1960, but – although his record for career goals was not broken until the winter of 1963 – in his last few seasons he was overshadowed by the all-round magnificence of Detroit's Gordie Howe. By nearly any standard, Howe is the finest hockey player in the game's history, and one of the most remarkable athletes of any time. Each of the qualities illustrated in this book, from strategy to speed to strength, Howe brings to the hockey rink in abundance.

Perhaps the only way in which Howe has not lived up to the standards of Morenz and Richard is in his lack of colour: for all his great athletic gifts, and for all his quiet, personal charm, Howe on or off the ice exudes about as much passion and individuality as an assembly-line, Big Three automobile. Yet, in his own way, he has been equally as dedicated to hockey as Morenz and Richard. His calm excellence on the ice is as much the result of hours of studious practice as of his natural abilities. And in this way he has been a standard-bearer for the sports of his time.

The years of Howe's dominance were the years of hockey's greatest success as a business, and the tenor of those years was reflected by the personality, or lack of personality, of the players. Where Maurice (The Rocket) Richard had seemed to relish his public feuds with the panjandrums of the NHL as much as he relished scoring goals, the grey-flannel figures who came after him – led and typified by Howe – have seemed reluctant to say anything in public or private that might endanger their next contract with a hair-oil company. "Knocking the game," as the league has come to call it, seems nearly as serious a sin to the modern player as losing was to Howie Morenz. The early 1960s in sport have been, with a decreasing number of exceptions, the age of a grim, calculated, commercial determination to win, and in many professional sports – as, certainly, in hockey – a lot of the colour and some of the joy have been drained from the athletes and the athletics.

It would be difficult, not to say naive, to be so optimistic as to report that the age of the super-commercialization of sport is now over. Big-time spectator sports are still very big business indeed. But they are also games. And at the end of Canada's first century it is possible to spot signs of a renewed interest among the athletes in the sporting side of sports. It is here where Hull, hockey's new dominant figure, serves as a clear symbol.

Hull combines some of the elements of all his predecessors, from the speed of Morenz and the instinct for goals of Richard to the strength and control of

Gordie Howe. But he has brought a quality of his own to the game. In the winter of 1964, when Hull was off on the most spectacular opening of a season by any player since Richard himself – thirty-three goals in the first thirty-six games – one of the authors of this book happened to be in Montreal and dropped in on the Rocket for a visit. Richard had recently been named a vice-president of Le Club de Hockey Canadien, and he was occupying a neat, handsomely appointed office in the Forum. He had put a few pounds onto his playing weight of a hundred and eighty, but his wrists still looked powerful enough to launch one of his characteristic, whistling backhands on goal, and the fire in his eyes was, obviously, only banked. At one point in the conversation, his visitor asked him for an assessment of Hull. Would Hull ever reach the pantheon of five-hundred-goal scorers as yet populated only by Howe and Richard? (No other player has scored four hundred.) The Rocket paused for a moment, as if wondering whether he ought to say what was on his mind. Then he said, "No. I don't think so. I don't think any of the younger players ever will. With me, when I was playing, everything was hockey. I never thought about anything else. Howe the same. The young players today, they don't work so hard at it. Their minds aren't on hockey all the time. They're interested in too many other things. They're not as hungry as we were. Hull probably *could* score five hundred goals, but I guess he'll burn himself out before he does."

To anyone whose experience of Hull is confined to reading about his phenomenal scoring streaks or about how he is able to lift his Chicago teammates, this candid judgment of the young superstar by the old one may seem harsh. But to anyone who has watched Hull – the sports pages' Golden Jet – on his finest nights on ice, or observed him cutting his swath through life away from the ice, Richard's judgment rings true. Hull at his best expresses a sheer joy in hockey. He skates with the abandon of a prairie twelve-year-old set free on a frozen river. He grins with delight, booming out the league's most ferocious slap shot. Although he is a remarkably clean and gentlemanly player, he sometimes seems to belt the opposition just for the thrill of the contact. And although he is a thorough-going and dedicated professional, he seems to get his greatest pleasure from the pure motion and excitement of the game. Away from the rink he follows his own interests – from farming to fast boats to scuba diving – with the same swashbuckling enthusiasm he brings to hockey. Hockey is his profession. But it is only his profession. It is not, as it was to the men whose tradition he carries on, a religion. He is, in other words, a professional amateur, an amateur in the big time.

It would, of course, be too much to expect that all the hockey stars of the future will have either the ability or the inclination to follow in Hull's pattern. (Although there are some young players with a similar zest; Montreal's Bobby Rousseau and Boston's Teddy Green are two of them.) But the fact of Hull's emergence puts a crack in the fortress of unadulterated commercialism that the National Hockey League, at the end of sport's Gilded Age, has come to represent. And, to the extent that Hull plays the game for the game's sake – and not for his honour or his wallet – he stands as a clear symbol of the new age of Canadian sport, the new age of amateurism.

The original amateur: when the McGill rugger team played the Harvard soccer team in the '70s, football was born.

FOOTBALL	THE CENTURY'S BEST	
Chosen by	*Best team*	EDMONTON ESKIMOS/1955
a	*Best backfield*	PARKER/KWONG/BRIGHT/MILES/LINDLEY
national poll	*Best lineman*	JOHN BARROW
of	*Best quarterback*	BERNIE FALONEY
sports	*Best player*	JACKIE PARKER
editors	*Best coach*	POP IVY

HOCKEY	THE CENTURY'S BEST
Best team	MONTREAL CANADIENS/1959-1960
Best line	HOWE/ABEL/LINDSAY
Best goalie	BILL DURNAN
Best defenseman	DOUG HARVEY
Best player	GORDIE HOWE
Best coach	DICK IRVIN

Picture Credits

Order of appearance in the text of pictures listed here is left to right, top to bottom. After the first recording, principal sources are credited under these abbreviations: Alexandra Studio, AS; David Bier Studios, DB; Michael Burns Photography, MB; Canada Wide Photo, CW; Central Press Photos Ltd. (from Miller Services), CPP; Ralph Greenhill Collection (from Miller Services), RG; Newton Photographic Associates, NA; Notman Photographic Archives, McCord Museum of McGill University, NPA; The Public Archives of Canada, PA; Toronto Star Syndicate, TS.

Cover Don Newlands.
1 Notman Photographic Archives, McCord Museum of McGill University.
2 Robert C. Ragsdale.
4 NPA.
6 Alexandra Studio.
8 Ralph Greenhill Collection (from Miller Services); RG.
10 Paul Duval; Paul Duval; Sports Hall of Fame, Canadian National Exhibition.
12 AS.
13 AS; AS; AS; Newton Photographic Associates.
14 David Kimpton.
16 AS; No credit; Toronto Star Syndicate (from Miller Services).
17 David Kimpton; AS.
18 Michael Burns Photography; AS.
19 AS; Werner Wolff, from Black Star.
20 Canada Wide Photo.
22 The Telegram, Toronto.
23 CW.

25 Don Newlands.
26 Howard Anderson; Central Press Photos Ltd. (from Miller Services).
28 Dr. Joseph B. MacInnis; Don Newlands.
29 AS; AS; MB.
32 Don Newlands.
33 Don Newlands.
34 CW.
36 AS; Windsor Star.
37 AS; CPP; AS.
38 Stewart Sherwood; CW.
39 CW; TS (from Miller Services).
40 David Bier.
41 NA; Hans Zander.
42 The Sun, Baltimore.
46 Jack Marshall.
48 The Public Archives of Canada; Jack V. Long.
50 AS; AS; TS (from Miller Services); AS; Alberta Government Photograph, from the Ernest Brown Collection.
51 David Kimpton.
52 John Little.
54 AS.
55 AS.
57 TS.
58 Dave Portigal.
59 Paul Rockett; Mirrorpic (from Miller Services).
60 Ken Bell.
62 AS; CW; AS; AS.
63 Canadian National Exhibition.
64 Paul Duval.
67 H. W. Weyerstrahs.
68 AS; Central News.
69 AS; Miller Services.
70 Ted Grant; Don Newlands.

72 Henri Rossier.
73 David Kimpton.
74 Caufield and Shook Inc.
77 MB.
78 John Richmond.
80 No credit; DB.
81 Wide World Photos (from Wheeler Syndicate); David Kimpton.
82 TS; AS.
83 AS;
84 AS.
85 TS.
88 Don Newlands.
90 DB.
91 AS; TS (from Miller Services).
92 DB; Don Newlands.
94 PA.
95 No credit.
99 Hans Zander.
100 TS (from Miller Services).
101 Horst Ehricht.
102 AS; Brown Brothers.
103 AS; TS.
104 AS; TS (from Miller Services).
107 PA.
109 AS.
110 Carlos Marchiori.
112 Claude Lance; AS.
113 AS; AS.
114 Wide World Photos (from Canada Wide); CW; Paul Gélinas.
116 AS.
120 The James Collection of Early Canadiana.
121 Wide World Photos (from Canada Wide).
123 Horst Ehricht.
125 NPA.
126 CW.

PRINTED AND BOUND IN CANADA

TEXT TYPE: New Times Roman

TYPOGRAPHERS: Howarth and Smith Monotype Limited
T. H. Best Limited

PAPER: Webcoat

LITHOGRAPHY: Litho-Print Limited

BINDING: *case printed by* Sampson Matthews Limited
case made by The Ryerson Press
bound by T. H. Best Limited